MORE
HERBS

Twelve Wondrous
Plants For:

extra nutrition
improved health
natural beauty

Carol R. Peterson

Published by Mountain Garden Publishing, Inc.
P.O. Box 98
Snoqualmie, WA 98065

Illustrator and Cover Design: Shaun E. Wolden
Copy Editor: Connie Chaplin
Technical Editor: Bob Lilly

Printed in the United States of America
First Printing, May 1999

Library of Congress
LC 99-90021

Publishers Cataloging in Publication Data:
Peterson, Carol R.
        More Herbs You Can Master: 12 Wondrous Plants
        For: extra nutrition, improved health, and natural beauty

        Includes Index and Glossary
        ISBN 0-9639620-1-9
        1. Herbs 2. Herb Gardening 3. Cookery (Herbs)
        4. Herbs-Utilization 5. Herbs Therapeutic.

TABLE OF CONTENTS

Note: For your convenience, each chapter in this book is made up of thirteen sections. Each of these sections is identified by its recognizable icon or symbol.

The sections are as follows:

1. Botanical Name

2. History

3. Type

4. Description

5. Planting And Care

6. Harvesting

7. Preservation

8. Propogation

9. Other Uses

10. Medicinal Uses

11. Culinary Uses

12. Recipes

13. Other Notes

ACKNOWLEDGEMENTS _____

I give my greatest thanks to Connie Chaplin, my copy editor, and
Bob Lilly, my technical editor. They were usually ahead of me in
their editing and always accomplished a very professional job.
A special thank you to Shaun Wolden my graphic designer, lay-out
person, cover designer, illustrator, web-site maker and the many
other hats that he wore. He really came through for me. Thanks to
Monica who's help has been invaluable with her computer skills.
Thanks to all of my wonderful readers who did outstanding jobs in
clarifying my material and making useful and insightful comments
throughout the text. Those readers are Debbie Arenth, Monica
Barbuscia, Marcia Barnett, Cecelia Bouglais, Erick Haakenson, Lisa
Harkins, Pam Jones, Linda Larion, Trina Parsons and Pam Teller.

Also, thanks to all of my students and clients who have encouraged
me greatly since my last book appeared in 1994. They have waited
patiently through my three back surgeries until I could get back to
my writing in earnest. I am grateful to all of my assistants and
friends who help me get out my mailings and volunteer in many
capacities in my one-woman business.

I really appreciated the informational meetings with Debbie and
Ron Arenth of Fall City Farms, Ted Andrews of HerbCo
International, and Paula and Erick Haakenson of Jubilee Farm
for vignettes and other information for this book.

Lastly, a big thank you to my husband, Charles, who always
encourages me to pursue my goals no matter how crazy they may
be at times. As you see, it takes many persons to create a book,
it never happens by a single individual.

Carol R. Peterson

INTRODUCTION _____

A garden is the mirror of a mind or a creation that was once vaguely imagined. In making my garden, I experience a sense of awe of God and what can grow from tiny seeds. My garden gives solace to my soul and merriment to my heart. A garden is a plan for order out of chaos and a human association with the divine. The unfolding beauty in each season of the year has its own meaning and richness. My herb garden is my favorite garden, although I also have rose gardens, perennial gardens, a vegetable garden, my wildflower bed (made from a twin bed) and several shade gardens. The herb garden is not only the best year around garden but has so many useful plants.

Rob Proctor and David Macke state in their book, Herbs in the Garden, that: "If you can cook with it; garnish a salad with it; soothe a burn or scratch with it; make a tea from it; soak in the tub with it; perfume your sheets with it; kill a bug with it; make a potpourri, sachet, wreath, or something else good-smelling with it; weave, dye, or spin something with it; scour pots or wash with it; worm your pet with it; formulate oils and lotions to beautify your body with it; cast a spell with it; or make a big mess involving a glue gun, wheat stalks, and raffia with it - it's an herb."

Any plant used for culinary, fragrant, or medicinal purposes is an herb. Botanically, an herb is any plant that does not possess a persistent woody stem and dies back to the root each year. Even though woody plants have medicinal or culinary uses, they are herbs according to the second definition. Botanists estimate that there are between 200,000 and 800,000 members of the plant kingdom. How many can be considered herbs by our first definition? About 80,000 plant species can be documented as folk medicines worldwide.

Herbs can be found in the earliest recorded history. Just as today, they were used to enhance the flavor of food, repel insects, improve air quality and cure the sick. In the seventeen hundreds, two physicians studied the herbal lore in the New World. They took differing views of the healing power of herbs. One found them quite useful and the other did not. While the herbal healers struggled with proponents of established medicine, chemists were studying the herbs to duplicate them for use in medicines. And so it remains today. There are two lines of thought on using herbs for healing. Just as in the past, there are "herbals," or books that describe the plants and how to use them for medicinal cures.

The idea of herbs supplying the deficiencies of the body which cause illness, originated with Paraclelsus, an alchemist who called active components of herbs, "essential oils", because he believed they contained the plant's essence or a concentrated version of all the characteristics of the plant. Chemists have now identified thousands of compounds that they classify as essential or volatile oil. Essential oil is particularly rich in the mint family that includes many popular herbs. In addition to supplying us with pleasure for the nose and natural medicine, these chemicals also have herbicidal, fungicidal, pesticidal, and generally antibiotic activities.

There is less chance of side effects from herbal medicines than standard drugs. Most herbal medicines have been out there for centuries. They wouldn't have lasted that long if they didn't work. Most modern medicines are on the market for five or six years and then they're gone. What do you think that means?

Essential oil from herbs can penetrate the body and cause actual physiological effects. They also have an emotional effect. Our sense of smell is tied to emotions, so different fragrances can elicit different emotional responses.

Herbs have long been relied upon for culinary, cosmetic, and medicinal use. They are not only aromatic and attractive, but also health giving, and valuable in both the home and garden. As Americans seek a healthier and more natural lifestyle, there has been a resurgence of interest in these most generous of plants, for cooking, household products, alternative medicines and cosmetics.

Growing your own herbs is also very economical. When we compared the cost of buying fresh herbs of the most popular kind, at the supermarket with buying herb seeds and plants for the garden, we found a savings of more than $100 a year. Herbs are very easy to grow so you don't have to do too much to reap great benefits.

The tongue only tastes sweet, sour, salty, and bitter. The taste buds can detect the flavor only when the substance is dissolved, such as in saliva. However, the aroma of plants and foods cause us to perceive that we are actually tasting. For instance, garlic is pungent, nutmeg is spicy and mint is cool. Training your taste buds to define the flavors of each herb is a fun and versatile endeavor. By brightening other flavors, fresh herbs play an important role in your cooking repertoire. They are one of the essential ingredients for boosting flavor in low fat, low salt recipes.

Herbs can bring to mind a sunny day, a delicious dish, a happy time - all with the power of fragrance and flavor. Herbs are the ultimate high-yield garden plants. You don't need a lot of space to grow them because they don't take up much room. When using them, a little bit of fresh herb goes a very long way. Just a few leaves or sprigs from one of these hardworking little plants is all you need to pump up the flavor of any recipe, and transform the finished dish from ordinary to outstanding.

I hope you will read about the twelve herbs I have chosen in this, my second book. They are fascinating plants that can hold your interest as a wonderful and productive hobby for many years to come.

Carol R. Peterson

ANISE HYSSOP

My Wonderful Bee Plant

ANISE HYSSOP

What first attracted me to this magnificent herb was the swarm of bees surrounding it. Now I know bees love many plants, but this one seemed to have something very special.

I grow the anise hyssop plants for three main reasons: the long-lasting blooms from mid-summer to the first frost, the delicate taste of the leaves and blossoms, and for the beauty of watching the bees, butterflies and hummingbirds have fun and nectar all summer long.

 ## BOTANICAL NAME _____

Agastache foeniculum or _Agastache anethiodora_ (an old name) with as many as 30 members of this family is sometimes known as giant hyssop. It is also called fennel giant hyssop because of its height, blue giant hyssop because of its flower spikes, and licorice or anise mint because of the flavor. Since anise hyssop is one of the few original American herbs, a prairie flower with lovely heart-shaped leaves, it is very easy to grow.

This herb does not resemble hyssop or anise or licorice, though its flavor is anise-like. All the common names refer to another plant, hyssop - _Hyssopus officinalis_, a Mediterranean herb with needle-like aromatic foliage. This hyssop herb is nothing like that of the _Agastache_, or anise, _Pimpinella anisum_, an aromatic and sweet herb that makes a soothing licorice-flavored tea and is a member of the _Apiaceae_ (or carrot) family.

The name _Agastache_ (pronounced ag-uh-STAH-kee) comes from the Greek words, agan, meaning "very much", and stachys, meaning, "spike". This plant really does have an abundance of terminal flower spikes that are in bloom throughout much of the growing season. The species name, _foeniculum_, means, "fennel," another herb that smells anise-like. The common name, anise, is from the anise seed-like smell and taste of the leaves, and "hyssop" is from the squarish stem, which is similar to that of the herb hyssop which is a member of the mint family, also known as *Lamiaceae*.

Blue Spike Anise Hyssop – *Agastache foeniculum* – is a vigorous perennial, blooming the first year from seed. This fragrant plant is equally useful as a fresh or dried cut flower. Its long-lasting, feathery spikes keep coming until hard frost on sturdy plants 3-4 feet tall and 18 inches across. It makes a great fragrant herbaceous hedge. The flowers are dusky blues to violet and are loved by bees and butterflies alike. As I cut the flowers when they are in bloom, the bees don't even bother me, as they are so intent on their nectar gathering business.

White Anise Hyssop – *A. f. 'alba'* – is similar to the dusky blue, but has white terminal spikes and a lighter green overall cast. White sibling to the blue spike hyssop, this hardy and productive perennial is equally valuable fresh or dried. Its long-lasting, showy blooms on sturdy 3-4 foot plants make an excellent herbal tea especially when used along with lemon verbena (another of my favorites discussed in a later chapter). This plant is not as bushy but is a good plant for a white garden, especially because of the fragrance. This variety comes somewhat true from seed.

Wrinkled Giant Hyssop – *A. rugosa (Korean Mint)* – is native to Asia. *Rugosa* means "wrinkled" and this wrinkled-leafed hardy perennial will grow to 5 feet. It has a lovely mauve, purple flower and is distinctively mint-scented. Its mid-green, oval pointed leaves make a refreshing tea. *Rugosa* is a denser and smaller version of anise hyssop and begins blooming later. It is somewhat short-lived but does self-seed. The stems are usually white and hairy on the upper part. This plant blooms from August through November. Indigenous to East Asia, Japan, China, Korea and eastern Siberia and Taiwan, this iced tea classic is grown for its economic potential. It grows in moist grassy places in mountains, valleys and along streams. The leaves and roots are used in Chinese medicine as well as for a flavorful tea.

Mosquito Plant or **Rio Grande Anise Hyssop** – _A. cana_ – is a native of New Mexico and Texas with rosy-purple, pink tubular 1-inch long flowers and gray leaves. _Cana_ means, "gray", and this is a half-hardy perennial and less vigorous plant growing 2-3 feet. With a good mint fragrance it is reputed to repel mosquitoes when its leaves are rubbed on the skin. It is not common in the trade because of its difficulty to propagate. You should rely on softwood cuttings rather than seed. (See the propagation information.)

Mexican Giant Hyssop – _A. mexicana_ – has slender, upright stems with light green foliage and long flower spikes. Flowers are generally clear pink to crimson or purplish with a eucalyptus scent. They attract Oregon swallowtail and yellow monarch butterflies. It is erratic from seed but cuttings usually propagate this variety. It has many flower colors and fragrances.

Toronjil Morado – _A. barberi 'tutti-frutti'_ – is a lemony, mint/citrus flavor hyssop, which grows to 3 feet with fuchsia to hot pink blossoms and a lemon scent. _Toronjil Morado_ means, "purple balm" in Spanish and is usually a half-hardy or tender perennial This plant can also be known as Tutti-Frutti. There is a variation in color and foliage, and sometimes even lack of scent or fragrance. The flower spikes are quite tasty and very colorful in flower salads when mixed with calendula and nasturtium. As a potted plant, it grows 3-4 feet tall but lacks winter hardiness; therefore, I recommend it not be exposed to temperatures below 25° F.

Arizona Giant Pink – _A. barberi_ – is one of the hardiest pink anise hyssops native to Arizona and New Mexico. This variety may get a light powdery mildew in hot, dry weather but is usually mildew free. Flowers have no taste but the foliage scent is reminiscent of catmint. This robust plant grows to about 3 ½ feet and prefers full sun with good drainage.

Apricot Sunrise – _A. aurantiaca 'Apricot Sunrise'_ – has tubular, burnt-orange colored blooms which are loved by hummingbirds because the spikes are up to 18 inches long with 1-½ inch tubular flowers. It reaches 2-3 feet with gray-green foliage. This is a good choice for a middle border plant with outstanding color and my personal favorite.

Firebird – _A. 'Firebird'_ – is a 2-4 foot plant with dark maroon foliage and coppery-orange flower spikes. This tender perennial blooms all summer with pungent scented foliage. Leaves with a distinct mint fragrance are used for hot or iced tea. _Firebird_ is easy to propagate from cuttings.

 ## HISTORY

Anise hyssops are native to central North America and East Asia found growing on prairies and plains. It has been found in north-central, central, and southwestern United States in dry thickets, plains and barren areas. The herb was gathered by the pioneers as a decorative flower, and was earlier used by northern plains Indians as a beverage tea. The infusion was also used as a sweetener. The flowers were often included in Cree medicine bundles, and the Chippewa used the root for coughs and respiratory problems. The Cheyenne utilized an infusion of the herb for chest pain due to coughing, colds, fevers, and most importantly, to correct a dispirited heart or weak heart. It is interesting that both the Asians and American Indians used anise hyssop for heart conditions. Perhaps with more testing we will find some further wonderful uses for this beautiful herb.

 ## TYPE

Anise hyssop is a robust, erect and attractive hardy perennial in most of its species. The plants die back in the late fall and go dormant until spring. This member of the mint family does not have the same invasiveness in the garden as mint although they have creeping rootstock. I have planted several varieties in the same bed and they do wonderfully together without intermixing. Most varieties are hardy to zones 4-5.

DESCRIPTION

Robust and attractive, these highly ornamental plants have strong upright stems with dense spikes of small flowers. These hardy herbaceous perennials grow in zones 4 to 9 in a variety of soils, but require much sun. Its anise-scented toothed leaves are short-stalked, ovate to triangular with a pointed tip and a sharply toothed margin. Anise hyssop grows 2-5 feet tall and with a spread of about 12 inches depending on the variety. They begin to branch after about a foot in length. Long-lasting spikes of flowers with a sweet aroma are up to 6 inches long and 2 inches wide shaped like baby ears of corn, and bloom from June through the fall. The sweet aroma and flavor make them excellent for hot or iced tea. The colors of the spikes range from deep mauve, magenta, white and greenish yellows to vivid reds, apricots, and even hot pink.

They are generally hardy to 15° F, and sometimes lower, depending on soil, drainage, snow cover, whether established or new plants, and whether or not they are in a raised bed. Anise hyssop neither tastes nor smells like the herb hyssop, but does have a sweet licorice taste.

PLANTING & CARE REQUIREMENTS

Being a prairie herb, anise hyssop likes drained rich, loamy soil to produce lush plants. Full sun is preferable because the herb likes warmth for 6 hours a day, but it will grow in light shade as well without stretching for the light. These easy-to-grow herbs like two parts garden or potting soil, two parts peat, one part sand, and one part compost or composted cow manure as an ideal seeding home. Sow seed in rows at least 12 inches apart and thin to 18 inches when they are 2 inches above ground. These plants will bloom all summer outdoors, but are not too happy indoors. They do fine in a pot on the patio or in a container at least 10 inches in diameter.

All varieties of anise hyssop complement and enhance the garden in companion with white or silver plants. The larger varieties are wonderful in the back row and the smaller ones can be used in the middle of a planting bed. They will die back in late fall and go dormant until spring. They are remarkably drought tolerant, dependable, infrequently bothered by insects but can be susceptible to green aphids when grown in the greenhouse. Only the two-spotted cucumber beetles seem to bother them in the garden, but they don't cause much damage. Even slugs pretty much ignore these plants - probably because of their strongly aromatic foliage.

 ## HARVESTING

Individual leaves and flowers can be harvested regularly throughout the summer and used fresh. Herbs are best cut in the morning when the dew is off the plant and the sun is just beginning to warm up. This is the time that the volatile oils are at their highest peak. When harvesting or cutting herbs, always use a clean knife or scissors that are sharp. Dull blades will damage the plant and reduce the quantity of the next crop. If you wish to harvest the seeds for later planting, wait until the heads turn brown and the seed ripens. In late autumn, cut back old flower heads and woody growth to ground level.

 ## PRESERVATION

Anise hyssop preserves well, keeping its familiar, much-enjoyed flavor and aroma as well as its color. Cut branches and hang in bundles to dry. Rubber band six to eight stems together and hang upside down in a cool, dry, dark area using a paper clip shaped in an S-hanger. Cut flowers for drying just as they begin to open. At the first sign of the seed falling, pick and put upside down in an open paper bag.

Cut leaves and flowers may also be dried in a dehydrator (see the Glossary), or in an oven that has been heated just to 200° F. and then turned off. Leave the oven door open and check the herbs frequently. They should be crisp when dried. Place the leaves as whole as possible into jars with tight-fitting lids. Label carefully as herbs tend to look alike when they are dry. Store in a dark cupboard - never above the stove! Use moisture-proof containers, as any moisture will cause the herbs to mold. Light will cause the essential oils to dissipate. (See Glossary.) Several bunches of the cut herbs can be dried throughout the season.

Another method for drying anise hyssop (and other herbs as well) is to use a microwave oven. Strip the leaves from the stems and lay in a single layer on a paper towel in the oven. Set microwave on high for 30 seconds, then turn leaves over and set for another 30 seconds. Check every 5 seconds to prevent burning. Over time the magnetron tube may be ruined if it is not shielded from microwaves that have nowhere to go when the moisture is evaporated and moist air is vented off the oven. You can add a small amount of water in a microwave-proof container in the oven to prevent any long-term damage. Microwave and oven drying are my least favorite methods of preserving herbs because it is so easy to overcook them and destroy the delicate volatile oils.

 PROPAGATION _____

Seeds, cuttings or root divisions are methods used for propagating anise hyssop.

Seeds may be sown in the spring or fall. Since light is preferred for germination, sow the seeds shallowly and just barely cover. They will germinate in 7-14 days and usually 70% of the seeds will germinate when sown directly into the soil. Small fine seeds need warmth to germinate so 65°F. is an ideal temperature. Of course, the seeds may be planted earlier in the greenhouse. Fall seeds will remain dormant until early spring. Young seedlings are easily transplanted, and even the mature plant transplants with ease at any point in its growth cycle. Don't place plants outdoors until the spring temperatures have warmed up.

Seeding can also be done directly into a pot. Cover the seeds with perlite and wet lightly and they should germinate within 10-20 days. They can be sown outside in autumn when the soil is still warm, but young plants will need protection when they peek through the soil. After your first crop of anise hyssop, the plants will self-seed on their own. Although, for some reason, my success with self-seeding is very limited. This is certainly the easiest way to increase your stock!

A. cana and *A. barberi* can be propagated from stem cuttings either in the spring or early fall. Cuttings of soft, young shoots can be taken in spring when all the species root well. Cuttings should be taken at a leaf node, cut at a 45° angle with a sharp, clean knife. Treat the cut stem with a hormone, such as Rootone and pot into a 50% perlite or sand and 50% peat mix. After a few weeks, tug at the tops of the plants to see if they have rooted, or look at the bottom of the container to see if roots are showing. The cuttings should be strong enough to plant out in the early autumn. After they have rooted, pot them and store in a cold frame over winter. Semi-ripe woodcuttings can be taken in late summer.

In the second or third year, division of the creeping roots may be done in the spring when the plants are just above ground. To propagate the plants in this manner, either dig up the whole plant or separate with back-to-back spading forks or remove sections from the roots and transplant to another spot.

 MEDICINAL USES _____

Anise hyssop has both an energizing and a cooling effect. Native Americans brewed anise hyssop flowers and leaves into a tea as a remedy for coughs and for respiratory problems as well as for cleansing. A decoction made from the roots also works well for respiratory cleansing. The Chippewa tribe used hyssop leaves

mixed with animal fat (bear grease) as a dressing for burns.
For minor burns, crush fresh anise hyssop leaves and swirl in an
equal part of aloe vera gel; apply to the skin and cover with a
bandage. It will feel cool at first but when the burn begins to feel
hot again, reapply the salve. Having a strong anti-fungal effect, the
leaves are applied as a poultice for sores of the hands and feet.
As an herbal steam, it really works to ease congestion of the nose
and head. It also stimulates gastric secretions, increases digestion
and relaxes blood capillaries.

In China, the aerial parts of *A. rugosa* are harvested in late summer
or autumn when the plant is beginning to flower. The whole herb
is dried in the shade or the stems can be cut into slices for using
fresh. The dried herb is the Chinese herb 'huo-xiang' and is used
in prescriptions for pain of angina, heatstroke, headache, fever,
and tightness in the chest, and to increase appetite, allay nausea,
and treat diarrhea.

 OTHER USES _____

The anise hyssop plant makes lovely dried flowers for wreaths,
floral displays or potpourri. Dried spikes left in the ground will
provide food for birds, as they will pick the seeds right out of the
spikes. This is yet another herb that can be used for moth
prevention by drying and adding to small bags in your cupboards
with linens or woolens.

 CULINARY USES _____

In the kitchen, there are many uses for anise hyssop that do not
need an actual recipe. Try some of these ideas. Steep a perfect cup
of herbal tea by adding 3 Tbs. of bruised fresh leaves (or one Tbs.
dried) to one cup of boiling water and steep, covered, until the tea
is light green and fragrant, about five minutes. It is essential to
keep the volatile oils from escaping, so keep the tea completely

covered while it steeps (a tea cozy helps to keep the pot warm or simply use a saucer over a cup). Strain the tea before drinking. Serve hot or cold. This fragrant tea of anise hyssop can be used to sweeten foods without adding sugar. Discard the leaves and use the tea to poach halved fresh peaches. Or make a dried fruit compote by simmering one cup of dried apricots in two cups of the tea until tender, about six minutes.

Press a dozen fresh anise hyssop leaves into the crust of a cheesecake before filling and baking for a very fragrant and delicious dessert. Use the flowers to garnish fruit cups, to sweeten fruit salad or melon, iced beverages, herbal iced tea, or to sprinkle on salads. Try adding a quarter cup of fresh anise hyssop leaves to a green salad. Add rinsed, fresh leaves to baked quick bread like muffins. Try some homemade 'aioli' for steamed shrimp or fish. (Aioli is a rich sauce with an egg yolk base. See the Tarragon chapter for a good recipe.) Dried flower tops can be crumbled over custard or bread pudding desserts.

Make herbal vinegar using sherry vinegar, peaches and anise hyssop leaves and flowers; or rice wine vinegar with fennel, Mexican marigold flowers and anise hyssop. Both are wonderful as splashes in soups or in salad dressings.

Honey produced from the plant is good quality, light in color and slightly minty in taste. This is one of the reasons that beekeepers frequently grow anise hyssop, and it is also one of the highest producers for honeybees.

 RECIPES

Herbed Butter

Add 2 Tbs. fresh, minced anise hyssop leaves to ¼ lb. unsalted butter, softened. Press with the back of a wooden spoon to mix well and add 2-3 drops fresh lemon juice. Roll in plastic wrap in 2-inch logs and refrigerate until firm. Unwrap and roll in a mixture

of chopped anise hyssop flowers. Wrap again and chill. Cut into
¼ inch slices right before serving. (Unsalted butter is always used
with herbal butters, because the salt in regular butter can
overwhelm the delicate taste of the herbs.) These butters may also
be wrapped in freezer-wrap and be kept frozen.

Anise Hyssop Lemonade

Infusion:
2 ½ cups water
1 ½ cup granulated sugar
¼ cup fresh anise hyssop leaves and flowers (coarsely chopped)

Combine the water and sugar in a medium saucepan. Bring the
water to a boil, stirring to dissolve the sugar. Add the anise hyssop
and remove from the heat. Cover and let the infusion cool to room
temperature. Strain and discard the flowers and leaves.

Lemonade:

Combine 4 cups of water
1 cup strained freshly squeezed lemon juice
Ice cubes
6-8 springs of fresh anise hyssop for garnish

Pour the infusion into a glass pitcher and add the water and lemon
juice. Stir well, adding additional sugar if desired. Refrigerate until
chilled. Just before serving, stir the lemonade again and fill the
pitcher with ice. Pour into chilled glasses and garnish each serving
with a hyssop flower sprig.

Pear Tart

1 ½ cups coarsely chopped anise hyssop leaves and flowers
2 cups half-and-half
3 large ripe pears; pared, cored and halved
½ cup cold butter
3 oz. cream cheese
1 cup flour
⅓ cup sugar
1 ½ Tbs. cornstarch

2 egg yolks
Pernod or other liqueur, optional
3-4 sprigs of hyssop flowers

Combine leaves and flowers and half-and-half. Bring to a simmer.
Remove from heat and allow it to steep for 2-3 hours covered. Lay
pears, flat side down, in a buttered 9-13 inch pan. Cut butter and
cream cheese into cubes. Combine in a food processor with flour.
Whirl mixture until it holds together. Press dough evenly over
bottom and sides of an 11-inch tart pan with removable bottom.
Bake on low rack in 375° F. oven with pears on the above rack.
Bake until crust is golden and pears turn brown, 20-30 minutes.
Cool. Strain and discard the leaves from the half-and-half. In a
saucepan, mix sugar and cornstarch, then stir in the cooled half-
and-half. Stir over medium-high heat until barely boiling. Stir some
of the cream into the egg yolks, then add the yolks and cream back
to the pan and stir 1 minute. Stir in Pernod if desired. Pour hot
anise hyssop cream into crust. Set pears, rounded side up, in cream.
Let cool, cover lightly and chill 8 hours or overnight. Before
serving, scatter anise hyssop florets between the pears and place
a small leaf cluster in the center of the tart. Serves 6-12.

Fruit Skewers with Anise Hyssop
½ cup vodka or fruit juice
1 cup fresh anise hyssop leaves
Lemon juice
3 cups mixed fresh fruit chunks
(Bananas, strawberries, pineapple, cantaloupe)

Mix the vodka and hyssop leaves (slightly crushed) with 2 Tbs.
fresh lemon juice and marinate for several hours. Skewer onto
wooden skewers alternating the fruit. Place hyssop flower atop
each skewer. (You may also use skewers of dried lavender or
rosemary stems.) This is a great first course that I use before a
barbecue when I am escorting guests around my herb garden.

Anise Hyssop Apple Tart

For the crust:
½ cup flour
½ cup whole-wheat pastry flour
2 Tbs. sweet-cream butter (or canola oil)
⅓ cup buttermilk
20 fresh anise hyssop leaves.

Toss the flours into a food processor. Add the butter in small pieces or the oil and whiz until the mixture is the texture of cornmeal. With the motor running, add the buttermilk and whiz just until a ball of dough forms. If the dough doesn't form a ball in about 6 seconds, add a splash of water. (Or use a bowl and cut in butter with a pastry blender; then add buttermilk and stir vigorously.) Spray an 11-inch tart pan with non-stick cooking spray. Press the dough evenly into the bottom and up the sides of the pan, then scatter the anise hyssop leaves over the dough and press them in. Refrigerate the crust for about an hour; then bake at 375° F. about 15 minutes.

For the filling and glaze:

4 medium baking apples; peeled, cored, halved and thinly sliced
1 large egg
½ cup buttermilk
3 Tbs. all-fruit apple butter
¼ cup flour
2 Tbs. all-fruit red currant jelly

Arrange apple slices in the warm crust. Combine the egg, buttermilk, apple butter, and flour in the processor and whiz until smooth. Pour over the apples and smooth with the back of a spoon. Bake until the filling is firm, about 30 minutes, remove the tart from the oven and immediately brush on the currant jelly, which can be heated to spread better. Serve warm or slightly chilled.

Anise Hyssop Honey Butter

½ cup honey, unflavored
¾ cup softened (unsalted) butter
2 Tbs. chopped anise hyssop flowers

Cream honey and butter together. Add chopped flowers and blend carefully. This is wonderful on morning biscuits.

Anise Hyssop & Almond Cookies

1 cup butter or margarine
½ cup sugar
2 cups flour
¼ tsp. salt
¼ tsp. almonds, ground or 1 tsp. extract
2 Tbs. of minced anise hyssop flowers and leaves

Cream butter and sugar. Add salt, almonds or extract and flour. Chill dough. Form into 1 inch balls and roll in sugar. Press with cookie stamp or bottom of glass dipped in sugar. Bake at 350° F. for 12-15 minutes.

Black Bean Salad with Anise Hyssop

2 cups cooked black beans, rinsed and drained
1 medium red tomato, cored and finely chopped
1 shallot, peeled and minced
1 Tbs. minced fresh chives
1 Tbs. minced fresh anise hyssop leaves
1 tsp. anise seed, lightly crushed
1 Tbs. balsamic vinegar
1 Tbs. olive oil

In a medium bowl combine the beans, tomato, shallot and herbs. In a small bowl whisk together the vinegar and oil. Pour over the beans and toss well to combine.

Anise Hyssop Steam

For a stuffy nose and head, crush ½ cup hyssop leaves and flowers with a mortar and pestle. Add the herb to a bowl filled with three cups of boiled water. Tent a towel over your head and inhale the steam for 5-10 minutes. Be careful that it's not too hot to burn you.

Facial Coolant

Steep 1 Tbs. of crushed anise hyssop leaves and flowers in half a cup of boiling water, covered, until cool. Then strain and swirl in half a cup of liquid witch hazel. Splash your face with the mixture after washing and before applying moisturizer. Or put in a spray bottle and spray your face from time to time throughout the day. This astringent tightens pores. Keep the mixture in the refrigerator. I use this when I am gardening in hot weather and it works wonders.

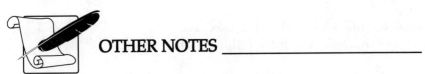

OTHER NOTES

Anise hyssop is a wonderful bee plant. The bees will remain in your garden as excellent pollinators all summer long. The spires of this plant attract many butterflies as well. The leaves and/or flowers can be dried for potpourri and sachets used alone or with any number of other herb choices. I especially like scented geraniums and lavender mix. The dried flowers also hold up well in fragrance and color in arrangements. Herb crafters use stems and flowers in their wreaths for many crafting ideas.

BAY LAUREL

The Noblest Herb Of All

BAY LAUREL

An ancient charm states, "Laurel tree, laurel tree; keep house and field lightning free." From laurel leaves, wreaths of victory were woven and worn to reward merit or to signify glory. Over 15 varieties are grown in Europe.

 ## BOTANICAL NAME _____

Laurus nobilis of the *Lauraceae* family is evergreen, and the leaves may be plucked in all seasons, including the middle of winter. This is the best form of laurel to be used in cooking. The tree is also called sweet bay, true laurel, bay laurel and Greek bay. The word *"bay,"* derived from old French *"baie,"* refers to the small, purple black berries on the tree. The tree is sometimes confused with cherry laurel, *Prunus laurocerasus*, which is poisonous. Cherry laurel also has evergreen leaves, but the fruit is bright red and much larger and not dusky-black like that of bay laurel.

Golden Bay – *Laurus nobilis "Aurea"* – can grow to 18 feet. Its small, pale yellow, waxy flowers come in spring and its green berries turn black in autumn. Its golden leaves can look sickly. This variety needs good protection in winter especially from wind scorch and frosts.

Red Bay – *Persea borbonia* – is not a true bay but grows native along the Gulf Coast of the United States. When dried, the flavor in the leaves dissipates, unlike true bay. It can be used in a fresh state, however, but is substandard to the true bay laurel.

Canary Island Bay – *Laurus azorica* – This evergreen perennial has reddish-brown branches.

California Bay – *Umbellularia californica* – should not be confused with bay laurel and should not be used in cooking. It contains toxic essential oils. This is sometimes called Oregon myrtle and has a close resemblance to bay laurel. It can grow to a height of 60-80 feet and has clusters of pale yellow flowers in late spring. Its very pungent 5-inch aromatic leaves, which resemble *Laurus nobilis*, can cause headaches and nausea when they are crushed. They smell like camphor with eucalyptus overtones and have a bitter flavor. Nursery people occasionally mistakenly substitute the California bay for bay laurel. Both trees are vigorous and beautiful, and the leaves of both are long, slender, fragrant and blue-gray-green. Put them side by side and you'll see that a sweet bay's leaf is firm and shiny, the California bay's duller, almost spongy. The difference in taste is dramatic. The ancients' sweet bay is a blend of smoke and sage. Chew on a fresh California bay and your mouth will be dazed with a pungency that amounts to something like clove overlaid with pine. After drying, the California bay leaves become sweeter, which is the opposite of what happens to sweet bay, or *Laurus nobilis*.

Willow Leaf Bay – *Laurus nobilis "Angustifolia"* – is also a perennial evergreen tree. This is a narrow, and long-leafed, variety growing to 23 feet.

Mexican Bay – *Litsea glaucescens* – is very similar in taste to bay laurel but has more of a eucalyptus scent with pine.

 # HISTORY _____

Bay trees are native to the shores of the Mediterranean region and Asia Minor. In warm climates, they may reach a height of 60 feet or more, but in cold areas they don't grow nearly as tall. In Europe, the bay leaves are cultivated and harvested from the wild. Bay is now commercially cultivated in Turkey, Algeria, Belgium, France, Greece, Mexico, Morocco, Portugal, Spain, the Canary Islands, Central America and the southern United States. Early Greeks and Romans created bay leaf wreaths to crown the brows of warriors and poets, of philosophers and statesmen, of vestals and emperors, as well as athletes; wreaths were a symbol of wisdom and glory. At the first Olympic Games in 776 B.C., laurel garlands were presented to the champions instead of gold, silver and bronze medals.

Nobilis comes from noble meaning "renowned." The Latin laureate means "crowned with laurels," hence, poet laureate. In medieval times, learned men and successful graduates were crowned with wreaths of laurel berries or bacca laurea, therefore the French term "bacclaureat" for those who successfully completed their second education. The term bachelor, awarded for passing a degree, is also probably a corruption of the phrase.

This beautiful shrub grows abundantly in Delphi, on the shores of the river Peneus. Apollo, the Greek god of the sun, prophecy, poetry and healing was smitten with love for the fair nymph Daphne, and pursued her relentlessly. Daphne, though, wanted nothing to do with Apollo. To help her escape his pursuit, Daphne's father, Peneus, changed her into a laurel tree. Apollo fell upon his knees before this tree and declared it eternally sacred. Thus the tree became the sign of glory, honor and greatness. Early Greeks dedicated the temple at Delphi to the god Apollo; they covered the roof with bay leaves to ward off evil spirits, and protect against disease and witchcraft. Witches and devils were held at bay if one stood near a bay tree. The death of a bay laurel tree was considered an evil omen. Apollo's priestesses ate bay leaves before expounding his oracles at Delphi. As large doses of bay induce the effect of a narcotic, this may explain their trances when they spoke.

In Greece, the aromatic branches of these lofty trees were much esteemed. The Greeks bound scrolls of important messages with bay branches to help ensure their arrival.

Until the Middle Ages, bay was used exclusively for decorative purposes. It was later used medicinally as well as for a most beloved culinary flavoring.

Romans used bay wreaths to guarantee long and happy marriages by baking wedding cakes on beds of bay. It was also taken to funerals, being good for the unborn, living and dead. Bay is used in many Biblical gardens as well.

The early colonists and pioneers used a bay look-alike (sweet bay) to flavor their meat and kept leaves in their lard and suet to prevent them from going rancid.

 ## TYPE _____

Bay is a hardy shrub or tree that is a perennial in warmer climates, tropical and sub-tropical areas, but is tender in colder climes. In my zone 7, I used to bring my potted bay into the basement for the winter, but since I now have a greenhouse it does much better there. It is cold hardy to 15° F.

 ## DESCRIPTION _____

This tall evergreen shrub has leaves that are shiny, dark green-pointed ovals, smooth and from 2-4 inches long and one inch wide. They are firm and leathery with a warm, pungent aroma that is especially intense if the leaf is snapped and the essential oil is released. Younger leaves are almost a pea green while the older leaves are a dark forest green. Small pale clusters of yellow, inconspicuous, waxy flowers with no petals bloom in the spring. Purple berries follow flowers in the autumn, which go black and hard when dried. When kept in a pot or tub, which I do in my Northwest garden, bay will likely grow no more than 10-12 feet. It can be espaliered against a wall with its branches stretching six feet to the sides.

 ## PLANTING & CARE REQUIREMENTS ___

When planting, find a sheltered sunny position for best results. Bay will also thrive in partial shade. Use a loose, moderately rich soil of sand, loam, peat and well-rotted manure and supply good drainage. Even though they are slow growing, they need ample water. Allow the soil to dry slightly between waterings. Give good liquid feed in the spring, fertilizing with liquid 10-10-10 at half the recommended strength. Check the soil 2-3 times a week in warm weather. The soil pH is ideal at 6.2. Even though the tree is

subtropical, it will withstand a frost or two during the year.
Bay is shallow-rooted and prone to frost damage. In severe winters
the leaves will turn brown, but come spring it may shoot new
growth from the base. To encourage this, cut the plant nearly down
to the base. Also, leaves are easily scorched in extremely cold
weather or in strong cold winds. Protection is essential especially
for bay trees less than two years old.

Bay trees are inclined to send up suckers around the base, and it is
wise to cut these off to make a better-looking tree.

The bay plants are practically pest free and will even keep insects
away from plants nearby. However, the most common insect
complaint that is serious is white wax scale, tiny insects that cover
themselves with hard, brown, shells and hold on for dear life,
sucking the plant's juices. They stick both to the undersides of
leaves and to the stems, sucking the sap. When the sooty black
spots (caused by this scale insect) appear, remove them with soapy
water and a soft cloth, or get rid of them by spraying with a
horticultural white oil emulsion. Once you see scale sticking to the
trunk, branches or the undersides of leaves, it is generally too late
to spray. Pick the insects off by hand using a cotton swab dipped in
alcohol. Sprays are effective only when the immature, microscopic
scale insects are running in late spring.

Bay trees make dandy tub specimens and may be trained as
standards on a central stem, with clipped, rounded tops like
helmets. They thrive on being trimmed in forms such as globes,
cones, standards, hedges, or various topiary shapes.

Small trees in pots are ideal for deck or patio. For a potted shrub, a
mix of sand, loam peat and well-rotted manure in equal portions
provides a good soil. Lightweight potting mix in a pot needs to
drain quickly and all but dry out between drenching. Add time-
release fertilizer to container plants in the spring or fertilize
regularly with a 12-12-12 formulation. Summer is a good time of the
year to plant one or two from a nursery to make the most of
growing time while the weather is still warm, for these trees are
slow to begin. Position in full sun with an hour or two of shade a

day, protected from wind and at least three feet away from other plants. Mulch in the spring to retain moisture. A potted bay tree presents two flushes of growth each year on regular stems: one in the late winter or early spring and again in the summer. Suckers, those shoots that grow from the roots independent of the main stem, often provide almost continuous growth if you wish to leave them on the plant.

As the tree grows, it can be transferred to a larger container. Or, it can be removed from a 7-8 gallon pot yearly to prune the roots, and the plant will continue to thrive in this size pot. I struggle to get mine to 5-6 feet in our zone 7 climate. But yearly, I remove the plant from the container, loosen the soil around the roots, and trim any roots that are circling the plant or are very long, and disinfect the pot before replanting with a new soil mix. Bay may remain in one pot for years if it is healthy and productive.

Bay prefers to be outdoors in warm weather, rather than indoors year around. Watch the light, moisture and fertilization. They are fairly drought-hardy after 2-3 years old but not in pots. A small bay can be brought in to a sunny window in the colder months. When inside fertilize once every two months. Bay also can be wintered over in the house in a pot where it will get morning sun, bright light the rest of the day and an even temperature between 60-70° F.

My first and only bay tree was started from a cutting and took many months to develop into something recognizable. After caring for the plant for seven years and taking it in faithfully every winter, I nearly lost it couple of years ago. The plant did not get watered regularly in the basement and leaves began to turn brown. After putting it outside in early spring, it still looked sick. As my husband and I were leaving for a week for an herb convention, we decided to remove it from the pot and put the whole shrub in the compost to deal with it later. When we returned, after heavy rains, we found that green leaves were beginning to grow. We placed the whole ball of the roots in a bucket of water for two days and, sure enough, it began looking great. It was dying of dehydration. It is now two years older and is a lovely specimen that I clip, prune and use regularly.

HARVESTING

Individual leaves may be picked from even a small tree, but don't strip them from the stem or take them from the bottom of the plant. Pick them early in the day by pulling down on the leaf to break the cambium layer and expose the node where another branch may grow. Being an evergreen tree, leaves can be harvested all year round. Use leaves at the ends of the branches or stems, pinching a piece of stem along with the leaves. This method will promote branching, as well as provide you fresh leaves. Cut back standard and garden bay trees in the spring to maintain shape and to promote new growth. Cut back golden bay trees to maintain color. These plants can be clipped back without harm.

PRESERVATION

Bay leaves dry well, holding their special perfume for years if properly stored. Cut the branches before midday, then snip off the leaves. To help retain a bright green color, they can be spread to dry in thin layers in an airy shady spot, and toward the end of the process pressed with boards to keep them from curling. Drying them in the sun will cause them to turn brown or black. They take about two weeks to dry. When they are quite dry, store them in an airtight container. These dried leaves will remain flavorful for up to six months if kept out of direct sun.

Drying can also take place in a dehydrator. I recommend the wooden variety, such as one called the Living Foods Dehydrator made in Fall City, Washington (see Glossary). I prefer this method because it's easier and faster, although the leaves do curl. Bay can also be preserved in vinegar. This not only makes flavorful vinegar but the leaves can be removed, rinsed in cool water and then used for cooking.

However, since I can use my bay fresh year around and certainly prefer the fresh flavor, I dry it only when making dried herbal combinations for gifts or for sale.

 ## PROPAGATION

The propagation of this plant is not for the fainthearted. The bay tree remains dormant throughout winter, but early in spring new green leaves start shooting. When these shoots have hardened after about eight weeks, the plant can be clipped back. Four-to-six-inch heel cuttings taken in late summer on semi-hard wood, or mature cuttings taken in early fall from fresh, green shoots usually yield a higher percentage of success. Snap the cuttings from the branches rather than using clippers. Cuttings are then stripped of the bottom leaves, dipped in Rootone (a hormone with fungicide) and planted in small pots of potting soil, sand or perlite. Place a plastic bag over each plant for humidity. A heated propagating mat is a great help in keeping the temperature constant and promoting root formation. Use a misting unit to maintain the leaf cuttings so they are well hydrated. Without roots at this point they can take in moisture only through the leaves. Check from time to time to see if new shoots are starting. When they do, (and this might take months) remove the plastic bag. If the parent plant sends out offshoots, dig them up or they will destroy the shape of the tree. Occasionally roots come with them and these then can be potted. They may take from 6-9 months to root, however. Don't plant new starts outdoors for at least a year or until the plant is one foot tall. One in 100 of these will probably take root.

Bay sets seed in its black berries, but rarely in cooler climates. Sow only fresh viable seeds (which are sometimes hard to obtain) on the surface of either a seed or plug tray or directly into pots in spring. They need a maintained temperature of 75° F. and should germinate within four weeks. Germination is erratic and may take place within 10-20 days, in six months, or sometimes even longer. Make sure the soil is not too wet or it will rot or mold the seeds.

Seed germination is chancy and the other methods of propagation are slow. The easiest way to have a healthy bay tree is to buy a young tree - they are a little pricey, but worth it.

 ## MEDICINAL USES _____

In medicine, the oil from the leaves and berries was recommended in treating rheumatism, hysteria and flatulence. For flatulence, indigestion or colic, use one ounce of bay leaves steeped in one pint of boiled water for ten minutes, strain and drink. This drink is also good for influenza and bronchitis. A powder or infusion of the berries was taken to improve the appetite and to cure the ague (chills and fever).

Culpeper, the seventeenth century astrologer physician, said, "It is a tree of the sun and resisteth witchcraft very potently." He also stated, "The oil made of the berries (can be pressed out by hand) is very comfortable in all cold griefs of the joints, nerves, arteries, stomach, belly, or womb."

Therapeutic uses include as antiseptic, painkiller, diuretic, emetic, narcotic, nervine and stimulant. Bay was used externally for sprains and bruises. The oil distilled from the fruits was once used as a liniment for sprains. The oil is anti-bacterial, anti-fungal and depresses the heart rate while lowering blood pressure. The leaves have been traditionally considered to be an astringent, aromatic, carminative, stimulant and stomachic.

Bay was used as often as garlic to protect against epidemics. Romans used bay leaves and berries for the treatment of liver disorders. Oil from the berries was dropped into aching ears. In the Middle Ages herbalists prescribed it to promote menstruation and induce abortions. It was also recommended for snakebites, wasp and bee stings, for colds, urinary problems, bruises, scrapes, and all sorts of ills. The Greek God of Medicine, Aesculapius, considered it a powerful antiseptic and guard against disease, in particular the Plague. In India, the dried berries were imported as a medicinal herb.

Bay has been described as an astringent for the skin. Add an infusion to a bath to relieve aching limbs. The essential oil has bactericidal and fungicidal properties. It contains eugenol, which has been found to have narcotic and sedative effects in mice. Using bay oil externally may cause dermatitis to some people but taken internally, appears to be safe. Bay is being tested for its potential in helping diabetics. So far they have found that bay beats insulin's ability by three times to break down blood sugar in test tubes.

 ## OTHER USES

Although some tests have shown that bay is not successful in keeping away insects, I have found that if I keep a leaf or two in my flour bin it does keep out weevils. Placed in open cupboards, the bay will keep away lots of little critters.

Bay leaves are used much like fennel seeds as a facial steam for troublesome skin. (See the Fennel chapter). An infusion as a skin lotion is good for troubled skin. It is also used as an antidandruff ingredient. Make a strong infusion and pour into bath water for a soothing soak.

Bay laurel can be made into wreaths for decorating. A culinary wreath on straw back or on moss back is easy to assemble and the leaves can be used right from the wreath. A bay laurel wreath is quite easy to make using a 10 inch grapevine, moss or straw wreath, several bunches of bay about 6-8 inches long, some florist wire and pruning shears. Use the wire to attach bundles of bay to the frame of the wreath. Continue with bundles every few inches going in the same direction. When the wreath is covered, you can leave it plain or add other assorted dried items such as wheat stalks, dried flowers and fruits, or garlic and dried hot peppers. Be creative, and most of all use the bay leaves after hanging the wreath on your wall.

Leaves are also good in potpourri (especially in winter). Put a sprig in a tussie-mussie for added fragrance. Oil from the bay is sometimes used as a perfume ingredient.

 CULINARY USES _____

Herbs should enhance the flavor of a dish, not overwhelm it. Bay is a good example of an herb that can easily dominate. This is one of the herbs most in demand. The aroma peaks between three days and a week after it has been picked. This brief drying time concentrates the oils just enough. Fresh leaves are the joyous inspiration of every cook, especially those who indulge themselves often in the French manner. Spanish and Creole cuisines also add bay to many essential dishes. In Morocco, bay leaves are used to line the cooking vessels in which the tiny pasta couscous (made from semolina) is steamed. It is strange that the Chinese, who traded with Asia Minor for thousands of years, do not use bay in their cuisine.

A portion of a dried bay leaf was all that was used in earlier times, but today a whole leaf adds a nice fragrance and pungency to a dish. Next to salt and pepper, bay leaves are the most used herb/spice in the American kitchen. Fresh leaves are not significantly stronger than dried. The special pungency of the leaves enhances the flavor of many foods, and besides being indispensable in most households, bay leaves are used commercially in flavoring various types of canned and preserved fish, meat and vegetables. A bay leaf is traditionally one of the four ingredients in a bouquet Garni´, the other herbs being a sprig each of thyme, marjoram and parsley; they are tied together and the bouquet is put into casseroles, soups and stews and removed after cooking.

Bay leaves on their own also flavor soups, stews and casseroles, as well as boiled, baked or steamed poultry, sausages, fish and meat, roasted game, tomato sauce, and pickles. They go into marinades (especially anything with tomato), and give a pleasing and unusual flavor to milk puddings, especially rice pudding. Add a bay leaf to the potato water for mashed potatoes or to water in which you cook rice. Remove the leaf, add milk or chicken stock and proceed as usual. This imparts a nice subtle flavor to the mashed potatoes. Add leaves to a jar of rice for an unusual flavor. These leaves are also excellent with lentils, beans or grains. Bay leaves can be added to herbed oils (see Sage) but should then be refrigerated. When preparing fish soup stock from fish bones, add a bay leaf or two.

Bay leaves are very good in combination with peppercorns, saffron, garlic, allspice, citrus and mustards. Whole fresh leaves are preferable to dried whole leaves, ground or crumbled. Here are a few ideas for you to try: rub the skin and cavity of poultry with mustard, then add a couple of bay leaves before roasting; place leaves on barbecue coals before grilling-especially salmon; when grilling beef or pork on skewers add a fresh bay leaf (dried leaves will crumble) in between each meat chunk; infuse red wine vinegar or cider vinegar with fresh leaves for use in salad dressings; toss a leaf into boiling water when cooking pasta. A bay leaf can be successfully used to replace salt in water when cooking pasta, rice or beans.

Bay brings an allspice type of spark to many foods. It has a sweet balsamic aroma, pervasive but not overpowering. A blend of balsam and honey with faint tones of rose, clove, orange, mint and other perfumes might best describe this aromatic herb. Its taste is sharp, slightly peppery with a medium bitterness. Historically, the guest who found the bay leaf in their serving was due to receive some minor or major fortune. Now, however, we remove it before serving. The reason for this is because the sharp edges of the bay leaf, even after cooking, can penetrate the wall of the esophagus. Even small pieces of bay should be removed.

 **RECIPES** _____

Bay/Sage/Thyme Vinegar
1 pint of apple cider (or white wine) vinegar
8-10 whole fresh bay leaves

Gently press the leaves in your hand to release the volatile oils.
Heat the vinegar to just below boiling. Add vinegar to a glass jar or
bottle (sterilized), and then add the bay leaves. Close with a cork or
other non-corrosive lid. Sit on windowsill in the sun for 6-8 weeks.
Don't remove the bay leaves. You may add other items as well,
such as, garlic cloves, rosemary or lemon zest or rind. Try the sage
and thyme as well using equal amounts.

Aromatic Baked Fish
Whole fish, cleaned and scaled (1 lb. per person)
Bay leaves
Vegetable oil
White wine
Herb or vegetable salt
Tarragon, chopped
Lemon slices, cut thinly

Lay the fish in a baking dish, place a bay leaf in the body cavity of
each, pour oil and wine over and around the fish. (Add 1 Tbs. of
each to every fish). Sprinkle with salt and just a little of the
tarragon, and arrange a couple of lemon slices on each fish. Bake in
a preheated oven at 375° F. for about 20-30 minutes or until fish
flakes easily. During cooking, baste the fish with the pan juices
from time to time. Serve hot.

Spiced Whole Grapes
2 lb. seedless white grapes
1 lb. raw sugar
5 oz. cider (herbed or fruit) vinegar
2 tsp. mustard seed

1 tsp. ground ginger
1 tsp. ground allspice
2 bay leaves
1 oz. powdered fruit pectin

Wash the grapes and remove the stalks and stems. Place the sugar and vinegar in a saucepan and add the mustard seed, ginger, allspice and bay leaves. Bring to the boil, and then simmer gently with the lid off for 15 minutes, stirring at intervals. Remove the bay leaves. Add the grapes. Sprinkle in the pectin, bring to the boil again and simmer for a further 3 minutes, skimming off any foam and giving the mixture an occasional stir. Remove from the stove and allow to stand for 20 minutes, stirring frequently to prevent a film from setting on the top. Spoon into jars and seal. Use within 4 weeks or freeze.

Bay Leaf Custard
4 ½ cups milk
6 sweet bay leaves
4 large eggs + 1 egg white
1 tsp. Worcestershire Sauce
Freshly ground white pepper & salt

Bring milk and bay leaves to simmer in heavy saucepan over medium heat. Simmer uncovered over low heat until reduced to 3-½ cups, about 20 minutes. Remove leaves. Rinse and wipe the leaves clean. Smooth a little oil inside 6 ovenproof cups (7-8 oz. each). Set one leaf shiny-side down in bottom of each cup and set on trivet in steamer over medium heat. Add hot water to the steamer to come up to bottoms. Combine eggs, egg white and Worcestershire sauce in measuring cup. If not one cup, make up difference with more egg white. Turn into bowl, add simmered milk and stir until blended, beating in as little air as possible. Slowly pour through sieve into clean bowl. Whisk in pepper and salt. Stir while pouring mixture into cups, holding leaf in place with handle of a wooden spoon. Lay foil over cups and cover steamer tightly. Steam; water barely simmering, until a metal skewer emerges clean, about 20 minutes. Center should quiver slightly. Cover cups loosely with foil and refrigerate. When cool, cover cups tightly. Unmold after 4 hours and scrape any custard off leaf.

Bread Pudding with Bay

⅓ lb. day old bread (most any kind)
½ cup chopped dried figs (or other dried fruit)
1 ½ cups whole milk, or skim
2 bay leaves
½ cup pure maple syrup
2 large eggs or 4 large egg whites

Crumble the bread into a souffle´ dish, mixing in the figs as you go. In a small saucepan, heat the milk and bay leaves until hot and fragrant, but not boiling. Take the bay leaves out of the milk but keep them. In a medium bowl, combine the milk, maple syrup, and eggs and beat with an electric hand mixer until well combined. Pour over the bread, patting down the top to level it out, then place the bay leaves on top. Bake in center of a 350° F. oven, uncovered, until firm, about 20 minutes. Serve warm with maple syrup, yogurt or saute´ed bananas.

Syrian Chick Peas, Rice and Bay

1 ½ cup medium grain brown rice
½ cup dried chickpeas (also called garbonzo beans)
3 cups water
2 bay leaves
3 Tbs. olive oil
2 large onions, thinly sliced
1 tsp. cumin seed, ground
2 cloves garlic, mashed
Juice of 1 lemon
2 Tbs. finely minced parsley

Soak the rice and chickpeas overnight in water to cover. Drain the rice and chick-peas and put them into a large covered soup pot with 1 bay leaf and 3 cups of water and simmer over medium heat until tender; about 50 minutes. Meanwhile heat 1 Tbs. of the olive oil in a large nonstick saute´ pan. Add the onions and cook over medium heat until browned and frizzled - about 7 minutes. Remove from the heat. In a small saucepan, combine the remaining 2-Tbs. oil along with the remaining bay leaf, the cumin seed, and garlic. Cook over medium heat and saute´ until fragrant, about 3 minutes. Remove from the heat. Add the cumin mixture, along with the lemon juice, to the cooked chickpeas and rice. Stir in onions to combine, taking care not to smash the rice. To serve, arrange the rice and peas on a platter and sprinkle the parsley on top.

Bay Hot Cross Buns

1 cup milk
3 fresh bay leaves (pick 3 days ahead for better flavor)
¼ cup honey
½ cup unsalted, melted butter
⅔ cup currants
2 ½ cups warm water
2 Tbs. active dry yeast
8 cups flour
2 large eggs
1 tsp. salt
½ cup water
1 egg white
Powdered sugar

Scald the milk with the bay leaves. Remove it from the heat and dissolve the honey in it. Let the bay steep in the milk for 30 minutes then remove the leaves. Soak the currants in 2 cups of the warm water for 15 minutes, then drain and squeeze the excess water from them. Discard the soaking water. Dissolve the yeast in the remaining ½ cup warm water. Sift 8 cups flour into a large bowl. Beat the eggs lightly and add them along with the salt and ½ cup water to the milk and honey. When the yeast is bubbly, add it to the flour along with the milk mixture, melted butter, and currants. Stir the liquid with a wooden spoon to incorporate about half of the flour. Remove the dough to a smooth surface and knead in the flour a cup at a time to form a soft, but not too sticky, dough. Knead for about 5 minutes after the last addition of flour. The final dough should be smooth, soft, and elastic. Place the dough in a lightly oiled bowl and cover tightly with plastic wrap. Let the dough raise in the refrigerator overnight or for as long as 24 hours, or let it raise in a warm place until doubled in size, 1-2 hours. Punch the dough down and divide it in half. Knead each portion for 3-4 minutes then cover the dough and let it rest until it is relaxed enough to roll, 20-30 minutes. Roll each portion into a long cylinder about 3-inch in diameter. Cut the cylinders into 2-inch slices and roll each slice into a ball. Place the balls on lightly buttered baking sheets. Cover them with a tea towel and let them rise in a warm place until almost doubled in size. Preheat the oven to 375° F. With a sharp knife; slash a cross in the top of each bun. Beat the egg white until frothy and brush each bun lightly with it. Bake the buns for 15-20 minutes until they are a rich golden brown. Remove the buns from the oven and let them cool on a rack to room temperature. Drizzle simple icing of powdered sugar and water over the buns.

Herbes de Provénce
2 dried bay laurel leaves (ground in spice grinder)
1 Tbs. dried thyme
1 Tbs. dried sweet marjoram
1 Tbs. summer or winter savory, dried
1 Tbs. dried rosemary
1 tsp. dried lavender buds
1 tsp. fresh fennel seeds, slightly crushed
2 tsp. grated and dried orange zest

Stir or grind all together and store in a tightly covered glass jar out of heat and light. Use on lamb and pork and in salad dressings.

Bouquet Garni
Parsley, Thyme and Bay Leaves
Use in a tea ball or cheesecloth tied close. Remove from pot at end of cooking time.

Herbal After-shave for Men
1 cup vodka
2 tsp. dried yarrow
1 Tbs. dried lavender flowers
1 Tbs. dried sage leaves
1 dried bay leaf

Mix ingredients together, and pour into a clean jar with a tight-fitting lid. Place the jar in a dark, cool place for two weeks. At the end of the two weeks, strain off the liquid and discard any solids. Pour the liquid into a clean container. To use, after shaving pour a small amount in your hands, and pat on your face.

Christmas Potpourri
3 cups fresh juniper sprigs (with berries if possible)
2 cups red rosebuds, dried
1 ½ cup bay leaves
¼ cup cinnamon sticks
2 Tbs. cloves
Small pine cones
10 drops of essential rose oil
3 drops of pine oil
6 drops of cinnamon oil
1 Tbs. orrisroot
5 whole dried rose blossoms

Combine first 6 ingredients in a large ceramic (non-metallic) bowl. Mix the oils with the orrisroot in a separate small bowl. Stir into the first mixture and put into a closed container to mellow for a few weeks, stirring occasionally. Pace the potpourri in an open dish and scatter the rose blossoms on top.

 ## OTHER NOTES _____

Bay is high in calcium, fiber, iron, riboflavin, and vitamins A and C. Do not consume the leaves except in a ground mixture, as I noted above; they may lodge in the throat.

People living on the Caribbean Island of Antigua believe that bay leaves offer protection from colds, flu and bad omens. Before a house is to be "exorcised" of evil spirits, three bay leaves are placed in each of the four corners of every room.

Bay is an excellent strewing herb because of its antiseptic and aromatic properties. Laurel oil from the berries is used in veterinary medicine. There is a specific recipe that is used for alopecia (baldness) but unfortunately I couldn't find it to try out its effectiveness. Nor did I have a willing candidate.

Another rumor or myth was that persons going to a party who intended to overindulge could remain sober by placing a bay leaf behind their ear.

NOTES: _____

BORAGE
Blue Stars Of The Garden

BORAGE

"I, Borage, always bring courage," was the opinion of John Gerard, the great herbalist. This was an old charm for courage that was recited while picking the blue blossoms of the lovely borage plant. The Cowardly Lion from the Wizard of Oz could have easily had all the courage he wanted just by drinking borage tea without making that treacherous trip through the Land of Oz. This herb is known as the herb of gladness for its exhilarating affect. However, it is in less demand than other herbs. I believe this is simply because people are not familiar with it.

 ## BOTANICAL NAME

Borago officinalis – Other popular names for this plant are beebread, herb of gladness, burrage, and cool tankard. The plant family is *Boraginaceae*. There are only three species.

Blue Borage – <u>*Borago officinalis*</u> – is the most commonly seen borage in the flower or herb garden. This tall plant has lovely blue or sometimes pink starflowers that are very unusual. It is so easy to grow that all gardeners should give it a try.

White Borage – <u>*Borago officinalis 'Alba'*</u> – This white borage is also a hardy annual to two feet tall with white star-shaped flowers. It has bristly, oval leaves and can be used the same as the blue flowered plant.

 ## HISTORY

Borage is indigenous to the Mediterranean countries and southern Europe, often in wastelands, but now is naturalized in North America and Northern Europe. The French *bourrache* (or Latin *borra*) is said to derive from an old word meaning "rough" or "hairy," which certainly describes the leaf. But the herb's beautiful pure blue flowers are its most extraordinary feature and may have inspired the color of the robes of the Madonna and charmed Louis XIV into ordering the herb to be planted in Versailles. The Welsh name translates as "herb of gladness" and in Arabic it is "the father of sweat" which seems appropriate since borage is a diaphoretic. Most credible however, is the Celtic word, borrach, which means "courage".

Old records say that borage originally came from Aleppo, although for many centuries it has been naturalized in many parts of Europe. The plant has a traditional reputation for relieving depression and lifting the spirits. The seventeenth century English author and epicure John Evelyn says, "Sprigs of Borage are of known virtue to revive the hypochondriac and cheer the hard student." The Greeks and Romans regarded borage as both a comfort and an imparter of courage. It was for this concept of courage that borage flowers were floated in cups given to the crusaders.

Even in later years soldiers would drink a brew with borage for courage and to ease their minds before marching off to war. Check out the recipe section for a recipe similar to this brew.

Borage was once a popular potherb with the leaves and roots often used as a vegetable and in a nourishing broth.

American colonists thought so highly of borage that they took the seed with them on their long adventure. A seed-order catalogue in America in 1631 listed borage seeds, where it was called burradge. Early settlers, too, drank borage in wine to calm them before long journeys - trying to contend with bandits, sickness and famine was enough to make anybody a little hesitant to travel.

The Pennsylvania Dutch, the Amish and Mennonites practice a form of natural healing called "powwow" using verses from the New Testament and various herbs. Each specialist would powwow in a different area; i.e. warts, coughs, birthing, etc. Borage plants were used steeped in brandy to calm the patient before healing could begin.

According to old wives' tales, borage was sometimes smuggled into the drink of prospective husbands to give them the courage to propose marriage. It was also a favorite among soldiers who added it to wine for courage in battle. Borage does bring a sense of elation and well being with some even calling it an anti-depressant. It certainly is beautiful enough to make the heart merry!

 **TYPE**

This is an annual plant that will continually self-sow during the warmer times of the year. This plant grows in all zones.

DESCRIPTION

Borage grows to be a large, stout annual with distinctive large leaves and clear blue delicate flowers. The blue, pink or white star-like flowers are edible, have five stamens and are carried on hollow, bristly, round, branching stems. Flowers bloom from early summer to mid-autumn. The center of each starflower contains black anthers in a cone shape, and the blossoms hang their heads downward. Each flower produces its fruit of four brownish-black nutlets that are the seed.

Both the stalk and the branching stems are covered with stubble of hairs. The broad, fleshy oval-pointed leaves are also hairy although not as prickly, while the clustered buds are covered with a softer down. The leaves are gray-green up to six inches long. The entire plant grows one to three feet tall. If the soil is very rich it can grow to be five feet tall. In spring, seedlings appear in the garden from plants the year before. I enjoy seeing these seedlings appear and, if there are too many, I just take the hoe and get rid of the unwanted ones.

The flowers on this plant attract bees to gardens. Once the plant is established, it usually looks after itself and will keep re-seeding, often in unexpected places. If not wanted, the surface-rooted seedlings are easily pulled out. Borage looks best when allowed to grow in clumps or drifts. The gray-green of the leaves and buds and the massed celestial-blue flowers are an attractive and restful sight in the garden

 PLANTING & CARE REQUIREMENTS__

Borage seed may be sown in spring and, in temperate climates, again in autumn. Sow seeds directly on the soil. Cover lightly and keep moist. Borage will tolerate many types of soil but a stony soil with chalk and sand imitates its native area. This plant, like many herbs, likes an open, sunny location or partial shade. Manure compost is the best fertilizer. Keep weeds at bay by hoeing regularly. Mulch to keep soil moist. Borage thrives in a well-drained site with a soil ph of 6.6 for optimum growth but will tolerate a range between 5 and 8. They germinate quickly and are full-grown in 5-8 weeks. Thin to two feet apart as borage occupies a lot of room.

If you are planting small pots of borage from the nursery, wait until all danger of frost has passed. Place a new plant in a hole twice the size of the herb's root ball, and water with warm water after filling the hole with soil. If borage plants need to be transplanted, do this when they are quite young as they develop a long taproot that needs gentle handling. Although borage falters in hot humid summers, it will continue blooming until the first frost and then wither to a black mass. It will die off at the first cold snap, but then self-seeds. When the flower head turns into seeds, collect or destroy them if you do not want borage plants all over the garden. Do not till in the flower heads or next year you will have a garden full of unwanted borage. Some years, it is the last flowering herb in the garden.

This is a good companion plant to strawberries as it strengthens the resistance to insects and disease. Don't let the borage overrun the strawberries, however! Because of the beautiful pink and light blue star-flowers, borage harmonizes nicely in a back border with other herbs in front such as chives, lavender and sage. Very few, if any pests or diseases bother this easy-to-grow plant.

Borage is not suitable for container growing indoors. However, when planted outside in large containers (like a half barrel), borage can be very effective combined with other tall plants or cascading plants, such as nasturtium. Use a fertile potting soil and fertilize every two weeks, keeping the plant moist and in full sun.

 ## HARVESTING

Borage can be harvested throughout the growing season in small quantities or in two or three large harvests during spring and summer. Another option is to make a couple of successive plantings. Harvest borage as it begins to flower and is just fully open. When picking the flowers, grasp the stem behind the sepals, then pinch and pull the black anthers and the entire corolla will drop into your hand. Deadhead flowers to prolong flowering season. Cut young leaves fresh throughout summer.

 ## PRESERVATION

Borage is certainly best used fresh but I have attempted to freeze and dry it. You may also wish to try crystallizing the flowers as in the recipe section. Pick flowers and leaves fresh for freezing or drying. Remove leaves from stems. You can peel the stems and chop them into a salad. For drying the foliage and flowers of borage, pick unblemished leaves and opened flowers after the dew has gone. Make sure leaves are not overlapping when laid to dry on flat racks. Or you may lay them flat on sheets of paper in a shady place. Fast drying under moderate heat is best because they tend to turn brown or black without good air circulation. When the leaves are dry and brittle, break them up with your fingers and store in an airtight container. Dry with care. Leaves do not dry very successfully. Keep the dried flowers separate, also in an airtight container. The dried leaves are fine in tea with other herbs and the dried flowers work well in potpourri.

To preserve flowers for later use you may also freeze them in ice cubes. These are great for fruit and iced drinks as well as in punch during the holidays. The best way to preserve borage flowers, however, is in vinegar or by crystallizing them.

 ## PROPAGATION

Borage is almost exclusively attained by seed since it germinates so quickly. In the fall, dropped seeds are sure to sprout into new plants the next spring. You may also sow two or three seeds in a 3½-inch pot in the greenhouse in very early spring, which will produce a salable plant in about three weeks. Sown in plug trays, they can be planted as soon as possible after hardening off. The seeds produce broad, large cotyledons similar in appearance to those of cucumbers.

Our friends Paula and Erick Haakenson of organic Jubilee Farm in Carnation, Washington have planted borage seeds over the years. Erick states that he has a bed of borage 60 feet by 30 feet. Each year the plants reseed so that now they have no room for weeds to grow. Erick would rather cut the plants down at the end of the season rather than weed. I agree!

MEDICINAL USES _____

Some of the ancient medicinal remedies used for correcting all kinds of maladies with borage are still valid today. Some uses, however, seem to be myths.

The seed contains potassium and calcium associated with mineral acids, while the stems and leaves include saline mucilage; the healing properties of borage are attributed to these saline qualities. It is related to another healing herb, comfrey, and both belong to the *Boraginaceae* family. The borage plant is comprised of 3 percent potassium nitrate. Because of the potassium nitrate, the dried herb can emit explosive sparks when it is burned.

As for the plant's ability to do away with sadness, dullness, and melancholy, we have to remember that the flowers and leaves were first soaked in wine or brandy to accomplish this purpose. Sufficient quantities of wine, without the borage, will achieve the same result - temporarily. The juice (taken from the leaves) however, has been useful in depression and anxiety.

Borage no more stimulates real courage than the potion in the square green bottle, which the Wizard fed to the Cowardly Lion in the Land of Oz. If you are expecting truly courageous results from a plant, try something else.

Borage seeds contain essential fatty acids and this oil has been effective for rheumatic or menstrual disorders and irritable bowel syndrome. The gamma-linolenic acid (GLA) rich oil extracted from borage seeds and made into capsules is available commercially for essential fatty-acid deficiency. This GLA deserves more medicinal research.

The plant's leaves and flowers contain saponins, mucilage, tannins, vitamin C, calcium and potassium. Hot borage tea is good in reducing fevers and restoring health after illness because it induces a sweat. It's a good remedy when colds and influenza are upon you, especially when these infect the lungs. As an expectorant it is also good for dry, rasping coughs. The flowers are used in cough syrups and can be combined with mullein flowers or marshmallow flowers.

Components of these leaves and flowers are good blood purifiers when used as a tonic for kidney ailments or pulmonary troubles. Post-operative heart patients have used a combination of borage and hawthorn berries to relax and to restore their spirits.

Both leaves and flowers stimulate the adrenal glands, encouraging production of adrenaline, the fight or flight hormone, which gears the body for action in stressful situations. This is probably why it was used by soldiers and believed to give them courage.

A poultice can be applied to the skin externally for eczema, inflammation and swelling. Juice the fresh leaves, mix with an equal amount of water, and use for irritated, dry skin or rashes. Oil of borage also makes a soothing lotion for dry, itching skin because it is an emollient. The GLA compound improves inflammatory skin conditions like eczema when taken internally or applied topically. GLA supplementation may have therapeutic promise in the treatment of atopic eczema.

A cup of borage leaf tea (hot or iced) is known for giving a lift after a hard day. However, prolonged use of borage is not advisable. Fresh leaves may cause contact dermatitis.

 ## OTHER USES

The flowers are useful for decorating confections. The whole plant is very attractive to bees. In fact, the garden sounds like high tension electrical wires when you are near the plants on a sunny day. This herb is frequently grown near hives for its plentiful sweet nectar. Be very careful when you remove a flower to be sure a bee is not attached.

Borage leaves and flowers can be used for dry and sensitive skin in a steam facial or facial pack (see the Recipe in the Fennel chapter).

 CULINARY USES _____

The whole borage plant reveals a delicate cucumber flavor, and for this reason the leaves and flowers are traditionally gathered to impart a cooling aroma to wine cups and cider drinks. Keep picked flowers in the refrigerator until ready to use. All parts of the plant bring a refreshing flavor to iced tea, lemonade or serve as a float in punch bowls. The pretty blue flowers improve flavor and delight the eye.

A handful of fresh leaves may be steeped in a quart of boiled water with a sprig or two of spearmint. Add a little honey and lemon juice, then ice, to make a cooling, soothing summer beverage with a calming effect. At summer's end, I make an ice ring with layers of borage, anise hyssop and other edible flowers. I use a gelatin mold ring and add just one-half inch of water at first and lay the flowers on top to freeze. When frozen, I add another half-inch, more flowers and continue until the ring is filled to the top frozen. We always use this ring on Christmas Eve in our cranberry punch.

The pretty blue flowers have been added to salads since Elizabethan times "to make the mind glad," a practice that modern cooks could follow. When borage leaves are finely minced they make a fragrant addition to salads, or remove the leaves from the succulent stem, peel the stems and put them in a salad. Another option is to peel, chop and use them like celery. The leaves can be eaten raw, steamed, or sautéed like spinach. Stems can also be peeled, chopped and added to apple and pear dishes.

Add chopped leaves to softened cream cheese, to yogurt or mayonnaise, or to an egg salad sandwich. With a dusting of salt and pepper, the leaves make a delicious substitute for lettuce.

The leaves are also very nice chopped in scrambled eggs. Fresh leaves are particularly good to use in a salt-free diet, as they are rich in mineral salts. Try them combined with spinach or added to ravioli stuffing. Whole young leaves may be dipped in batter, fried and eaten as a vegetable. They blend well with dill, garlic and mint and enhance cheese, fish, poultry, most vegetables, and salad dressings. Add chopped leaves when making pickles from cucumbers or beets.

The starry flowers of borage can be crystallized for decorating cakes and trifles, or used fresh as a decoration on sweets. (For instructions for crystallized flowers see the Recipe Section.) Euell Gibbons has recipes for borage syrup, borage candy, and jelly.

You really can eat these hairy little leaves. The hairs dissolve in the mouth. The older leaves are too fuzzy to eat raw, but they can be added to soup stock to impart a cool cucumber flavor. Add one-half cup borage leaves to one quart of simmering soup stock, and then use the stock to make creamy cucumber soup. The chopped leaves of borage make soup tasty and healthful. Add a handful of leaves when making chicken or fish stock. If you object to the fuzziness of the leaves, use them for flavor and strain them from food before serving. Chilled soups like the Vichyssoise recipe below and iced cucumber soup with minced borage leaves and flowers are excellent cooling summer dishes.

Warmed white wine vinegar with borage leaves and burnet flowers makes good vinegar.

 **RECIPES** _____

Borage Leaf or Flower Tea
Bring 8 ounces of water to a boil in a saucepan, toss in 1 tsp. dried flowers (or 2 tsp. fresh flowers), cover and simmer for 1 minute. Allow to stand for a further 3 minutes. Strain and drink. Or pour 8 oz. boiling water onto 1 tsp. dried borage leaves (or 1 Tbs. chopped fresh leaves), cover and infuse for several minutes. Strain. Do not add milk, but sweeten with honey if you desire.

I also like this in combination with lemon verbena and anise hyssop. This makes a very light, flavorful drink on a cold and blustery day.

Sangria with Borage

Large handful of borage leaves
3 sprigs rosemary
4 cups red wine (Cabernet, Chianti, etc.)
2 cups pure apple juice
3 tangerines, sliced
Borage blossoms

Place borage leaves and rosemary in a very large wide-mouthed jar
and use a pestle to pound them lightly until bruised. This will
release their fragrance so they can perfume the wine and juice.
Pour the wine and apple juice over the herbs and add the
tangerines along with their juice. Cover and let steep refrigerated
for at least 48 hours. The sangria will keep refrigerated for one
week. Strain and serve chilled with floating borage blossoms.

Borage Vinegar with Shallots & White Wine

See the Salad Burnet chapter
Also try Borage/Salad Burnet Vinegar with shallots

Salad Dressing with Borage

1 ½ Tbs. white wine vinegar
½ tsp. Dijon mustard
½ tsp. sugar
½ Tbs. lemon juice
Salt & pepper
½ tsp. each of chopped herbs (borage leaves, tarragon, lemon
verbena, dill)
1 clove garlic, minced
6 Tbs. olive oil

Mix together in a salad bowl in the order given and whisk.

Borage Butter

½ cup unsalted, sweet cream butter, softened
1 Tbs. borage flowers
1 Tbs. mint leaves, minced
1 tsp. dill leaves, minced
1 small clove garlic, minced
Few drops of fresh lemon juice

Mix all together in a mortar and pestle (or mash with the back of a wooden spoon). Place in tartlet pans and level the tops and freeze. Remove and place in zip-lock bags. This butter is particularly good on biscuits or cornbread.

Borage Flower Canapés
¼ lb. cream or goat cheese at room temperature
1 Tbs. finely chopped chives
3 Tbs. milk
1 large loaf of firm, dense bread (unsliced)
20 borage flowers
20 sprigs of other herbal flowers (anise hyssop, thyme, pineapple sage)

Add chives and milk to cheese and stir until smooth. This mixture should be spreadable without being drippy. Trim all crusts from the bread and slice into ⅓ inch slices. Cut slices into squares 2-½ inch x 2-½ inch. Spread cheese mixture on bread (not too close to the edges). Refrigerate covered with plastic for a few hours. Pick and clean, carefully, the herb flowers. Be sure the flowers have not had any pesticides or other sprays on them. After gently rinsing leave them in the refrigerator in a bowl of water for a few hours. Pat dry and place the herbal flowers attractively on the bread squares and serve right away or cover with plastic wrap and keep in refrigerator up to 2 hours.

Borage Soup
1 large handful of borage leaves (about 4 oz.)
1 lb. potatoes
3 cups milk
Salt and pepper to taste

Wash the borage leaves and chop them very fine. Peel and wash the potatoes, cut into small chunks, and cook in boiling water until soft. Drain the potatoes and mash them very smooth. Gradually add the milk, stirring until well blended. Place the saucepan over low heat, add the chopped borage and the salt and pepper and simmer for 30 minutes. Serve hot or chilled with a spoonful of sour cream or yogurt and a borage flower floating in the center of each bowl.

Vichyssoise with Borage Flowers

6 large leeks, cleaned, tops trimmed, leaving only white part
4 Tbs. butter
4 cups chicken stock (preferably homemade, unsalted)
3 medium potatoes, peeled and diced
2 Tbs. chopped very young borage leaves
1 cup sour cream (or ½ cup plain yogurt and ½ cup sour cream)
Salt and white pepper
Nutmeg
Borage flowers to garnish.

Slice the leeks into thin slivers. Melt the butter in a large saucepan, add leeks and sauté over moderate heat until softened. Add chicken broth, potatoes and borage. Bring to a boil and simmer covered for 35 minutes or until potatoes are tender. Strain the broth. Pureé the vegetables in a food processor or blender. Combine both and pureé. Chill overnight. Just before serving stir in 1 cup of sour cream (or combination) add salt and pepper and nutmeg. Serve in chilled bowls with borage flower garnish.

Borage Fritters

2 oz. unbleached or whole-wheat pastry flour
Salt to taste
1 egg
2 tsp. vegetable oil
2 Tbs. milk
3 small to medium-sized borage leaves for each person

Mix the flour and salt together in a bowl. Whisk the egg and stir it into the flour, then add the oil and milk and beat until the mixture is smooth. Take the borage leaves one at a time and dip into the batter, coating well, then fry in 2 Tbs. vegetable oil on both sides until golden. Drain on absorbent paper towels. Eat these fritters as a vegetable with roasts and grills or as a tasty accompaniment to fried chicken. The hairiness on the leaves disappears during cooking.

Shrimp Salad with Borage
Steam and shell 1 lb. of shrimp. When cool, add a peeled and sliced avocado. Toss with some lime juice and fruity olive oil and garnish with ¼ cup of borage flowers.

Crystallized Flowers
Pick several blue starry borage flowers and remove the sepal from the back of the flower. Be sure petals are very dry. Place on parchment paper laid on a small oven tray. Stir the white of 1 egg with a fork (don't beat it to froth), then using a small paintbrush, paint both sides of the petals with the egg white. A quick method is to dip petals straight into the egg white, coating them well with the fingers. Be careful you don't break them. Shake superfine sugar over the petals. (Run plain white sugar through a food processor to break it down to a superfine quality.) Turn petals over and sugar them again. Place the tray in an oven, turned to the lowest temperature and leave the door open. The petals will harden and candy in about 10-15 minutes; keep turning them and do not leave for too long or they will go brown. Store in an airtight jar or box between layers of waxed paper. These candied petals make a pretty decoration for a cake or cookies.

 OTHER NOTES _____

Dried borage flowers add color to potpourri and can be pressed for making stationary or other paper or packaging items. Children enjoy picking and stringing the flowers together as a necklace. Add borage blossoms to summer flower arrangements.

The painted lady and anicia checkerspot butterfly caterpillars especially like borage.

NOTES

DILL

More Than A Pickle Herb

DILL

Simple to grow and beautiful to look at, dill deserves a place in either a vegetable or herb garden. This herb has the tenacity to grow wild and fill all of your flowerbeds if you let it. This versatile culinary herb is one that beginning herb gardeners should always include. Dill comes from the Norse word, *'dylla'*, meaning to soothe or lull. Dill is a member of the *Apiaceae* or carrot family.

 ## BOTANICAL NAME _____

Dill – <u>*Anethum graveolens*</u> – is a very familiar genus of herbs. It has long been a favorite of Americans as an ingredient in the kitchen, whether gourmet cooking or just plain pickles.

Common Dill (also known as Bouquet Dill) – <u>*A. graveolens*</u> – is the most widely grown of the dill family. It blossoms early with large seed umbels and foliage for pickling. It is dwarf, compact, bushy and 1-½ to 2 feet tall.

Dukat Dill – <u>*A. graveolens 'Dukat'*</u> – is greener than most dill with a strong flavor and high oil content.

Superdukat Dill – <u>*A. graveolens 'Super Dukat'*</u> – is also known as Tetra Dill and also has a higher essential oil content and is greener than most dill varieties. Compared to Dukat, the flower heads are at a more uniform height and the plant is straighter and cleaner for easier harvesting. Its abundant foliage is perfect for salad use. It can also be grown for its seed to season various condiments. We sow in clumps rather than single plants.

Fern Leaved Dill – <u>*A. graveolens 'Fern Leaved'*</u> – is a dwarf dill, only 18 inches tall and slow to bolt. It was a 1992 All-America winner. Its very abundant dark blue-green foliage is a beautiful addition to the garden or excellent in limited space such as one per container. While it flourishes in the garden and will conveniently re-seed for years, it languishes in confined areas if planted too closely.

It germinates and grows quickly and may be planted after danger of frost, or year-round in mild climates.

Indian Dill – _A. graveolens 'Sowa'_ – is pungent and somewhat bitter and is grown in India and Japan. The fresh foliage is eaten with steamed rice and used to flavor soup. The oil is used in pharmaceuticals and the perfume industry. The fruits or seeds have a carminative effect so are used mostly for flatulence.

 ## HISTORY _____

Dill is native to the Mediterranean region, as are many other herbs. It is found in Southern Russia, Southwest Asia and Europe. It was familiar to the ancient civilizations of Greece and Rome. Dill is little used in the western part of the Mediterranean area but used daily in Greece, Egypt and the Middle East. Egyptian doctors used dill 5,000 years ago. Early Greeks and Romans hung bunches of the herb in their homes to freshen stale air and burned the seeds as incense.

Its popularity extends to Eastern European cuisine as well as being used prolifically in the Scandinavian countries, especially Sweden. This herb is now naturalized in some parts of North America and India. In the Middle Ages, witches used dill in magical spells to stave off storms. Banquet halls were decked out in floral dill bouquets and warriors coming home from battle would be crowned with fragrant dill garlands. It is referred to in early Saxon manuscripts, and it was often mentioned by writers in the Middle Ages, which demonstrates how old its reputation is as a soothing herb. This is one of the herbs most in demand by cooks in the United States.

Dill was used in Biblical gardens and was mentioned in the book of Matthew where it is suggested that herbs were of sufficient value to be used as a tax payment. The early American colonists called dill, "meetin' seed," because it was chewed for refreshment and to stop grumbling tummies during long church meetings.

TYPE _____

Dill is a hardy annual that is grown in all zones in the United States. Although an annual, it can self-seed if you do not remove all of the seeds in the fall. This annual will complete its life cycle in one growing season, going from seed to flower and then setting seed again on its large flat umbels.

DESCRIPTION _____

Dill has a long, thin spindle-shaped root called a taproot, much like a carrot. The stems or stalks are smooth, ribbed, hollow and have a bluish-green cast. When growing, dill and fennel look similar in the garden, but fennel is a perennial, has many stalks and its taproot is branched. Dill is smaller, with tiny yellow flowers and the foliage is finer and a deeper green in color. The single stalk springs up to a height of over three feet with a spread of one foot, but does not have the bushy habit of established fennel. When flowering, dill is recognizable by its flat, deep yellow, spreading blossoms, each consisting of many tiny, perfectly bunched posies on straight, fragile stalks. These complex flowers, although identical in form, differ widely from others of the same family in size and color. The seeds are ribbed, brown, flattened and elliptical and produced in great quantities and are high in essential oils. They have a pungent, bitter taste and retain their germinating capacity for three years. All parts of the plant are aromatic with a slightly sharp yet sweet flavor. The plant flowers June through August and the foliage may be used at any time.

PLANTING & CARE REQUIREMENT

Dill makes a good background to other herbs in the garden such as parsley and chives because of the lovely color and height. Dill prefers well-drained, fertile soil in full sun to partial shade. It likes a soil ph 6.0, a little on the acid side. It cannot tolerate frost and needs protection from wind. Keep the plants away from fennel as the seeds will cross-pollinate and their individual flavors will become muddled with the next year's crop.

Sow all seeds while the moon is waxing, and harvest when it is waning. These are the 'tried and true' times that have been used for centuries.

Directly seed dill in early spring (April to June) where the plants are to grow and flower. Cover the seeds to a depth of just ⅛ inch, as the seeds need some light to germinate. Germination rate is high and can take place in as little as 7 or as many as 21 days at 60-70° F. The time will depend on the warmth of the soil. Thin the plants to 12 inches apart when they grow to a foot tall. Individual plants may require staking. If you are growing the plant especially for the foliage, you can plant only 8-10 inches apart. If you plant every few weeks, you will have a steady supply all summer and into the fall. Dill likes 6 hours of sun per day and will do well as long as it is kept moist and well weeded. Choose a location protected from strong winds (or tie the stalks to a sturdy plant stake).

If you prefer to start the plants indoors in peat pots, begin 4 to 6 weeks before the last spring frost. Fill all trays or pots in advance, level the surfaces, and gently firm with a board. Water with copper fungicide to prevent damping off (plant wilt at the seedling stage) and allow draining until nicely damp, not wet. Sow the seed thinly and sieve more compost gently over the seeds to just cover. The general rule is to cover with a depth of compost equivalent to the size of the seed. Label with name and date and place the containers on a warm bed, covering with glass, plastic or newspaper if mist is not available in a sunny window. Make sure the compost does not dry out, but do not over-water. Plant the seedlings out as soon as there is no chance of frost and they are just a few inches high. If you wait too long and the taproots grow too lengthy, the dill gets upset and is likely to bolt and skip the leaf-producing stage altogether when it is transplanted. In climates that do not have severe winters, a second sowing in autumn, however, is also possible.

Dill likes cool weather and does not do well in the heat and humidity of southern climates where it dies out in mid-summer. You may want to plant dill near cabbage, onions and lettuce as a companion plant as it enhances their growth; or plant around the perimeter of a garden to attract bees. Pick a permanent spot as the plant is self-seeding and chances are good that new plants will shoot up every year if you let the flowers go to seed.

If conditions are crowded, aphids will appear. Good air circulation is essential. Use a liquid insecticidal soap for aphid control. In our Pacific Northwest area, the slugs love baby dill. I try to find the clusters of "pearls", or white eggs of the slug and destroy before they become adults. My search and destroy missions usually entail either chopping them in half with my trusty pruners or skewering them and putting them in the garbage. I know it sounds gruesome, but around here it's either the plants or the slugs.

I am an inveterate seed collector, especially of herb plants. Watching the new seedlings come up in the spring from the "Mother" plant is awesome. It's very satisfying to have free plants and seeds each year. (See the Propagation section for more on seeds.) If you plant early enough, seed heads should appear at the beginning of the summer after the weather is fully settled.

Dill grows indoors, but not as easily, and as in the garden still needs 6 hours of sun a day. The pot needs to be large enough to accommodate 18 inches of taproot space and lots of rooting room. Because it is rangy, it should be planted in a pot by itself. About every five days, check the soil for moisture. Water before it dries out completely. Use light fertilization every 3-4 weeks.

Overhead watering after plants reach two feet in height can increase the risk of powdery mildew infestation. Dill is sensitive to wind damage as well as hard rains during flowering and fruiting periods.

HARVESTING

Dill leaves are harvested just before the plant comes into bloom and plants set seed. In small quantities, the leaves can be picked for eating at any time after the plant has reached this maturity. You can begin plucking bits of leaf as soon as plants are 4-6 inches tall, but for maximum harvests, snip the leaves close to the stem about 2 months after planting. By harvesting regularly you will promote new growth and keep the plant reasonably compact.

The fruits or seeds of dill should also be harvested for their particular and special uses. The powers of observation come into play in seed collecting when you determine the right time. The time to pick the flower heads is when the flowers have mostly fallen away and the seeds are dry and look like they are about ready to open. Seeds can be harvested as soon as the tips begin to turn light brown. Those seeds on the lower side of the flower umbel will be ripe, while the others will ripen as they dry. If you don't want dill coming up everywhere in your garden (and probably your neighbor's too!) cut it back before the flowers drop their seeds. Harvest with sharp shears so that the stems are not damaged. Handle the sheaves gingerly to keep the seeds from falling off the flower head and into your garden. Cut the stems with enough length to allow them to be tied in a bunch and hung in a dark place. Spread paper beneath them to catch the dried seeds as they fall. If the seeds do not fall, you'll have to pull them off by hand. Seed heads can also be removed from the stalks and placed upside down in paper bags. A closed bag will cause mildew if the seeds are not perfectly dry at harvest. Put in a warm place for a week. After dropping into the bag, rub them between your palms to remove the husk The harvesting may begin when the flower heads start maturing in midsummer and go on into autumn. Some seeds may drop, which remind me of the almost forgotten practice in severe climates of mothering the seeds that fall - that is, leaving them where they lie on the ground and covering them during winter. Seedlings that have been mothered make the strongest and earliest plants, but in a very cold spring they should be protected or they may suffer.

In winter, dig up all remaining plants making sure all the seed heads have been removed before you compost the stalks, as the seed is viable and will produce in your compost bed. The whole plant should then be cut down and the seed drying completed indoors.

Do the harvesting in the early morning or in the evening. This will capture the highest essential oil content of both the leaves and the seed. If grown indoors the plant will get leggy, soft and prone to disease. You can plant in a pot outdoors in a very sunny location.

 PRESERVATION _____

Dill foliage can be preserved very successfully by freezing. It also can be dried but sometimes loses much of its flavor. For preserving the dill at season's end, leaves or fronds are picked when the plant is mature. Dill stems can be frozen intact and then simply snipped off with scissors. Return the remainder to the freezer immediately. I use 6-mil zip-lock bags. These are intended for freezer use and are not the sandwich type. After placing the dill in the bag, remove all the air and place bags in the freezer.

Although leaves don't dry well, they do have some color and flavor. Dill weed should be carefully spread to dry in a single layer at a temperature of 90° F. on fiberglass screens for a couple of days in a warm dark place. I use the Living Foods Dehydrator built in Fall City, Washington and have had it operating nearly constantly since 1972. (See the Glossary.) In this way, I can control the temperature. After the leaves are brittle, place them in an airtight way, I can control the temperature. After the leaves are brittle, place them in an airtight container. I use a storage cupboard that is dark, so it isn't as important to place them in dark jars. Hanging the stems in an airy, shady place may also dry the leaves. When hung to dry without temperature regulation, the dill may turn an undesirable brown color. When very dry and brittle store the leaves in an airtight jar. Dill weed and seeds should have relatively high essential oil content. Dried dill weed has limited uses because its aroma is fairly delicate; dill loses much in drying, especially if it is crumbled or dried for too long.

After collecting and drying the seeds, I shake them through a colander to remove most of the chaff and then store them in glass jars or in camera film containers, which are dark. (Be sure the seeds are completely dry before storing.) You can also insert little silica bags that sometimes come in pill bottles or shoe boxes. If you don't have that, you may place a little powdered milk in a tissue and insert it in the container to absorb any moisture that might be remaining. Otherwise, any moisture will cause the seeds to mold. Label your saved seeds with date and type.

If you have planted dill in a large pot as described earlier, you can bring a plant into the house to use fresh year around. Dill weed, as it is sometimes called, will last only a couple of days in the refrigerator in a glass of water before it droops and loses its flavor.

 ## PROPAGATION

Hybrid seeds are those that result from selective pollination to produce plants with tough skins that will ripen simultaneously and be resistant to disease. These seeds cannot naturally reproduce true-to-type and must be replaced every year. Heirloom seeds, on the other hand are open-pollinated seeds that rely on nature to spread their pollen and propagate their seeds. They generally produce hardier strains that are naturally resistant to pests and taste better. See the Glossary section for information on seed-saving organizations.

Direct seeding of dill in the garden is the best way to propagate for more plants. As noted under Planting & Care Requirements, a couple of different methods may be used. In any case, you will be very pleased with the success rate for these easy-to-grow and tasty herbs.

 ## MEDICINAL USES _____

Historically, dill has been used for treating coughs and headaches. The seeds are used as a carminative. Medicinally, only the seeds of dill are valued because of their oil content, especially the essential oil carvone.

Dill is well known for its beneficial digestive properties. Whole or ground, these seeds help with the assimilation of starchy foods (such as pastries, breads, pasta, and biscuits) and of certain vegetables tending to produce flatulence (such as cabbage, cucumber and onions). It is also very helpful to us in digesting stewed and baked fruit like apples, pears and quinces.

Try this recipe for flatulence (gas): Dill Seed Tea - bring 1 pint of water and 1 Tbs. of bruised dill seed to a boil. Cover, lower the heat and simmer for 15 minutes. Strain and drink hot or warm up to three cups a day. Keep leftover tea covered in a cool place and reheat the quantity needed each time. For other medicinal purposes and added calcium, make a cup of strong dill tea (1 Tbs. of dill seed, crushed, steeped for four minutes in a cup of boiling water). The flavor is a cross between fennel and caraway.

A cup of dill seed tea just before bed also induces sleep. It has been used for centuries as a nighttime drink for insomnia. In addition to this calming effect, it is also said to cure hiccups. Dill seed is also used as an appetite stimulant, especially in elderly people and has been used to stimulate milk production in nursing mothers. The seeds and leaves are used to relieve congestion in the chest of nursing mothers and for colic in their babies.

Dill seeds are helpful in bronchial asthma and in allaying nausea. When I was pregnant and had nine months of morning sickness, I used it regularly. Other medicinal uses of dill are for genital ulcers, hemorrhoids, and even neuralgia. With all of these uses, it's easy to see why dill has been a favorite in Chinese and European medicine for many, many years.

 ## OTHER USES

One of my favorite uses of dill seed is to sweeten the breath as a cure for halitosis. Just chew a few dill seeds and odor is gone! Making an infusion (strong tea) from crushed seeds and soaking your nails for 5-10 minutes can strengthen fingernails. Dill seed is used in sleep pillows to promote restful sleep.

Leaves of fresh dill make an attractive addition to indoor floral arrangements, but the water needs to be changed daily. Fresh dill can be used as background color on culinary wreaths and it dries well.

 ## CULINARY USES

Dill is one of my favorite herbs, as you will see by how many recipes I have given you in the Recipe Section. Dill complements so many different foods that your pantry or refrigerator should never be without it. There is a theory that when root vegetables are cooked with dill seed, the seed's vital essence, drawn from the sun, air and light, is released during the cooking process, balancing the vegetable's heavy root substance that was molded within the dark solidity of the earth. In any case, the dill seed improves the flavor and digestibility of hearty and healthy root vegetables.

Foods ranging from soups, pickles, fruit pies, seafood, cheese dishes, to many salads and certain vegetables all profit from the wonderful flavor of dill. Both seeds and leaves are used in flavoring foods, but the seeds are more pungent. Therefore, this sharper flavor is used in flavoring soup, lamb, stews, and grilled or broiled fish. Dill leaf can be used generously in many dishes as it enhances rather than dominates the flavor of food. Don't think only basil is used for pesto (meaning, 'to pound'); I have a great dill pesto recipe in the section below.

The seeds, leaves or both are found in baked goods of all descriptions, including breads, crackers, cookies, cakes and pies. It's also used regularly in sauces for poultry and vegetables, with meats, particularly in Russian and Eastern European recipes and to enliven simple egg or potato dishes. Dill also combines successfully with parsley or chervil to flavor the poaching liquid of chicken, fish and early summer vegetables. The flavor of the leaves is a mix of anise, parsley, and celery with a distinctive green bite on the sides of the tongue.

The aroma is a clean combination of mint, citrus, and fennel with a touch of sea air. The seeds taste predominately of caraway and anise. Because dill contains just two volatile oils (as opposed to rosemary with five), it goes well with many other herbs and food. The two oils have the familiar taste of celery and lemons, which are light enough to harmonize with, rather than overwhelm, delicate foods. While aniseed, caraway seed and fennel seed all have a similar sweetish pungency, the taste of dill seed is different: it is astringently aromatic, and may be used instead of the other seeds if preferred. The dry scent of the leaves is pleasing to most people, and may be substituted as a variation in dishes where you would use parsley, mint, basil or tarragon. For instance, a dill pesto is a great alternative to a traditional pesto of basil.

When adding dill to a favorite recipe serving four, use two teaspoons of freshly chopped dill or ½ tsp. per serving. These finely chopped dill leaves are particularly good in creamed potatoes, or in white sauce, cottage or cream cheese, fish dishes, omelets, chicken dishes, veal, salads, soup, tomato juice, vegetables, herb butter and vinegar. Try these fern-like leaves with vegetables such as carrots, cucumbers, cabbage, onions, cauliflower, parsnips, squash, eggplant, spinach, broccoli, turnips, green beans, and tomatoes. Dill's flowering yellow heads are often used in pickles and brines. For pickles, place a dill head, before it has set seed, in the filled jar and then sterilize in a canner. Pickles can be made from cucumbers, cauliflower, carrots, green beans and many other varieties or combinations of vegetables. I prefer to place an immature seed head in each jar because it gives a softer appearance.

Chop dill leaves into yogurt or sour cream for a vegetable dip or topping for baked potatoes. Dill seed in apple pie is delightful.

Dill seed has a dominant flavor with a pleasant tang, especially in Russian and Scandinavian cooking. Whole seed is preferable to ground, and fresh leaves are preferable to dry. Dill is also a good replacement for salt.

 **RECIPES**

And now my favorite part, some delicious and easy recipes for you to try.

Mustard Dill Sauce
1 egg + 1 yolk
2 Tbs. fresh lemon juice
2 Tbs. sugar
2 Tbs. Dijon mustard
1 tsp. grated lemon zest
½ cup chopped fresh dill leaves
1 cup safflower or canola oil

Blend egg and yolk until creamy. Add lemon juice, sugar, mustard, lemon rind and dill. Beat or process until smooth. Add oil in a slow, thin stream, with motor running. This will thicken when refrigerated. Serve on salmon, crab, shrimp or other fish.

Dill Aioli (Mayonnaise Sauce)

½ cup mayonnaise
2 cloves garlic, minced
2 tsp. fresh dillweed
½ tsp. salt
¼ tsp. white pepper

Combine all ingredients and let sit for at least one-half hour so flavors can meld. Use on potatoes, asparagus, tomatoes or other vegetables.

Dill Pesto

1 cup fresh dill weed
½ cup fresh curly parsley, with stems
1 large garlic clove
¼ cup freshly grated Parmesan cheese
3 Tbs. walnuts
1 tsp. grated lime zest
5 Tbs. olive oil
Salt and pepper to taste

Combine all the ingredients except oil in food processor bowl. Use pulsing action to incorporate. With machine running, slowly add the oil in a steady stream. Turn machine off, scrape down sides of bowl, season with salt and pepper. Store in refrigerator for a few days or in the freezer for a few months.

Yogurt and Dill Cucumbers

2 cucumbers (English style is best with seeds mostly removed)
10 oz. yogurt
1 Tbs. chopped green dill
Salt and pepper

Peel cucumbers if you wish or just score down the length of the vegetable with a fork. Peel the cucumbers thinly (remove a bit off each end) and slice them. Blanch in cold, salted water for 30 minutes. Drain well and rinse. Mix remaining ingredients together in a shallow dish and serve chilled over the cucumbers garnished with chopped fresh or dried dill leaves.

Mint & Dill Butter
(See anise hyssop recipe)
2 Tbs. fresh, minced dill and mint
1 clove garlic, minced
¼ lb. unsalted butter

Dilled Oil
Place 2 Tbs. chopped fresh dill and 2 cloves of garlic, minced, in one cup of sunflower oil. Shake and place in refrigerator. This should be used within four weeks to prevent botulism from forming. (Never give herb oils as gifts for this reason.)

Dilled Vinegar
Fresh dill leaves
3 cloves garlic left whole, but peeled
Nasturtium flowers, gently rinsed
1 pint cider vinegar

Place in a clean and sterilized pretty bottle with a non-reactive lid (like a cork) and place on a sunny windowsill for 2-3 weeks. (This product is very safe and does not need refrigeration.)

Dilled Tomato Soup
1 cup chopped onion (sweet variety if available)
3 Tbs. vegetable oil
12 ripe plum tomatoes, blanched, peeled and chopped
3 cups de-fatted chicken stock
¼ cup chopped dill weed
Ground black pepper
Several sprigs of parsley
Finely chopped dill and yogurt for garnish

Sauté onions in a pot for three minutes over medium-high heat. Add tomatoes, chicken stock, parsley and dill and bring to a boil. Season with pepper. Reduce heat to low and simmer for 15 minutes. Purée soup in a blender. Serve hot or cold with garnish.

Dill Seed and Pumpkin Soup
2 lb. peeled pumpkin
2 Tbs. raw sugar
Salt to taste
2 cups chicken stock
2 tsp. dill seed, slightly crushed
Pepper to taste
Yogurt or cream
Ground cinnamon

Boil the pumpkin with the sugar and some salt in barely enough water to cover. When soft, drain off the excess water and discard. Push the pumpkin through a sieve or food mill, or puree in a blender. Slowly add the chicken stock to the pumpkin puree, stirring well, and then add the dill seed. Salt and pepper to taste. Heat through on the stove and pour into bowls, putting a spoonful of yogurt or cream and a dusting of cinnamon on each serving.

Dilled New Potatoes
1 pound of unpeeled, new potatoes
½ cup of chopped, sautéed onions
2 Tbs. minced dill leaves
¼ cup herbal vinegar
⅓ cup olive oil

Boil potatoes until just barely tender. Sauté the onions and combine with potatoes. Sprinkle with a dressing of minced dill leaves vinegar and olive oil.

Cabbage Salad with Dill
1 small head of Chinese or other cabbage
1 large cucumber
6-8 scallions
Salt and pepper
4 Tbs. sunflower oil
2 Tbs. white wine vinegar (or rice vinegar)
4 hard-boiled eggs, peeled
3 Tbs. chopped dill

Wash and drain the cabbage and cut in thin strips. Peel the cucumber and cut in small semi-circles. Slice scallions using some of the green portions. Mix all together and add salt and black pepper. Stir in the oil and vinegar and mix thoroughly. Cut eggs in semi-circular slices and add to salad. Mix lightly add chopped dill at the same time.

White Bean Salad with Lemon and Dill
2 cups cooked white beans
½ cup minced celery
¼ cup minced red bell pepper
2 scallions (or green onions) finely chopped
Juice of ½ lemon
1 tsp. olive oil
1 clove garlic, finely minced
1 tsp. finely minced fresh dill

In a small bowl, whisk together the lemon juice, olive oil, garlic and dill. Pour over a mixture of the vegetables and toss well. Serve at room temperature.

Beets with Dill
1 ½ lb. small beets, cooked and peeled
2 Tbs. butter
⅔ cup sour cream
Sea salt and black peppercorns, ground
2 Tbs. chopped dill

Cut beets in thick slices. Melt the butter in a pan and cook the sliced beets gently until heated through. Add the sour cream and simmer for 2-3 minutes. Add salt and pepper. Stir in the chopped dill and let stand for a few minutes, covered, before serving.

Gravlax
(traditional Scandinavian dish)
1 ½ to 2 lb. Salmon; middle cut or tailpiece
1 heaped Tbs. sea salt
1 rounded Tbs. caster sugar
1 tsp. crushed black peppercorns
1 Tbs. brandy
1 heaped Tbs. fresh dill

Mix all ingredients (except salmon) and put some of the mixture into a flat dish large enough for the salmon piece. Place one piece of salmon skin-side down on the bottom of the dish. Spread more of the mixture over the cut side. Add the second piece of salmon, skin up, and pour over the remaining mixture. Cover with foil and place a plate or wooden board on the salmon. Weight this down with bricks. Place in the refrigerator for 36-72 hours, turning fish completely every 12 hours or so and baste with the juices. To serve, scrape off all the mixture, pat the fish dry and remove the skin, and slice thinly at an angle. Serve with buttered rye bread and a mustard sauce called Gravlaxsas.

Gravlaxsas
4 Tbs. milk
1-2 Tbs. Dijon mustard
1 tsp. mustard powder
1 Tbs. caster sugar
2 Tbs. white wine vinegar
6 Tbs. vegetable oil
3-4 Tbs. chopped dill

Mix the five ingredients together and slowly add the oil until you have a sauce the consistency of mayonnaise. Stir in the dill.

Dill and Garlic Bread
1 ¼ cup warm water
1 Tbs. honey
1 Tbs. active dry yeast
1 Tbs. olive oil
½ cup flaked rye*
½ cup flaked wheat*
⅓ cup oat bran
⅛ cup yellow cornmeal
1 tsp. minced dried dill (or 1 Tbs. fresh)
1 small clove minced garlic
1 ¼ cup all-purpose flour
1 cup whole wheat bread flour

Pour the water into a large bowl and stir in the honey and yeast. When the yeast has dissolved, stir in the oil. Add the rye and wheat flakes, oat bran, cornmeal, dill, and garlic and stir until blended. Gradually add the flour, ½ cup at a time until dough comes together into a ball and can be kneaded. Knead until smooth and elastic about eight minutes. Spray a large bowl with nonstick

cooking-spray and set in the dough. Turn the dough to coat it. Cover with plastic wrap and let dough raise in a warm place until doubled in size, about 45 minutes. Punch the dough down and set in a 9 x 5-inch loaf pan sprayed again. Cover the pan and let rise about 30 minutes. Spray the loaf with water for a crisp crust and bake at 375° F. on middle rack of oven for 45 minutes. Cool on wire racks before slicing.
*Available in health food stores.

Smoked Salmon and Cheese Hor d'oeuvres
½ lb. goat cheese
Freshly snipped dill fronds
¼ lb. smoked salmon (or other fish)

Form goat cheese into coins about the size of a 50-cent piece. Dip the tops in dill and refrigerate to very cool. Before serving, add a teaspoon of smoked salmon to the top of the dill. This is a great appetizer with crackers.

Dilled Ricotta Torte
1 cup whole almonds
1 ½ cups fine dry breadcrumbs
½ cup unsalted butter, softened
Salt
¾ lb. natural cream cheese, softened
1 cup Ricotta cheese
2 eggs
2 Tbs. half-and-half
⅓ cup snipped dill leaves
½ tsp. freshly grated nutmeg
1 tsp. grated lemon peel
Dill sprigs

Make a medium-fine meal of the almonds in the blender or food processor. Transfer them to a bowl and blend in first the breadcrumbs and then the softened butter. Season with about ¼ tsp. salt. Press the mixture on the bottom of a 9-½ inch springform baking pan and about 1-¼ inch up the sides.
Preheat the oven to 350° F. With an electric mixer on medium speed or with a food processor, combine the cream cheese, ricotta, eggs, half-and-half, dill, nutmeg, and grated lemon peel.

Blend the mixture very well and season with salt. Pour the mixture carefully into the prepared shell and bake for 1 hour and 10 minutes. Cool the torte to room temperature on a rack. Remove the springform ring and garnish the torte with dill sprigs. The torte may also be served chilled.

Dill Oil as a Lotion
Heat ½ cup olive oil or canola oil in a small saucepan over medium heat until just warm. Pour into a clean bottle to which you have added two tablespoon of dill seed, slightly bruised. Add a teaspoon of wheat germ oil as a natural preservative. Cover and steep in a cool, dark place for a week, then strain. Rub into hands, cuticles and nails while they are still damp for chapped hands and split nails. Good for the feet, too.

 ## OTHER NOTES _____

Although many other herbs and spices (such as basil, cinnamon, rosemary and tarragon) contain calcium, one tablespoon of dill seed contains 100 milligrams of calcium. Recommended daily allowance for healthy adults is 800 milligrams per day. Dill leaves contain magnesium, iron, potassium, phosphorus and Vitamin C as well as calcium.

Soil and climate greatly affect the quality and quantity of the essential oil of dill. Although the black swallowtail butterfly caterpillars especially like the dill plant, they should be encouraged because they are so beautiful when they reach their adulthood. I just plant enough dill for the caterpillars, too.

FENNEL

Flavor And Foilage For Fish

FENNEL

An old charm about fennel that is said to start a motorized mower is performed in this manner: hold the fennel in your left hand, salute the mower and say, "Mower, mower, finest of all, With this fennel, you'll purr, not stall." Now if this really worked, we wouldn't need those lawn mower mechanics.

 ## BOTANICAL NAME _____

Fennel is grown for its leaves, seeds and stems and is one of the herbs most in demand. The generic name, *Foeniculum*, derives from the Latin and Roman word *foenum* which means "hay," and refers to the foliar structure. *Foeniculum officinale* or *foeniculum vulgare* is considered wild fennel. In California this plant is sometimes referred to as wild anise. Also known as sweet fennel, it is a member of the *Umbelliferae* family that also contains carrots, parsley and, of course, dill.

Sweet Fennel – *F. vulgare* – is a stout perennial. This fennel is cultivated almost worldwide and is even found growing wild on sea cliffs and in waste places. With its gray-green color it grows to nearly five feet. It is cultivated for its leaf stalks - which taste similar to celery - as well as its gray-green fronds or leaves. The Italians are particularly fond of this variety and call it *'Carolsella.'* This variety is preferred for culinary purposes and is becoming more in demand. *Zefo Fino* is by far the best strain available as shown in numerous universities' trials.

Bronze fennel – *F. v. 'Purpureum'* – is a highly decorative form of fennel with bronze-red lacy foliage and a metallic luster. This plant is lovely in the background of a herbaceous border. It can be used in the same manner as the green fennel.

There are several other named red-leaved fennel including 'Giant Bronze' and 'Smoky'. Their flavorful leaves add that elegant, final touch to fish chowder or a fresh garden salad.

Florence Fennel or **Finocchio** – _F. vulgare azoricum_ – is sometimes called sweet anise or vegetable fennel. This is a smaller-growing annual (two and one-half to three feet) with many uses. The blue/green fernlike foliage, which is more delicate in flavor than perennial fennel, may be mixed with other greens in a salad, or cooked with fish, counteracting the oiliness of fish. Unlike sweet fennel, this variety forms a bulbous base of delicate anise flavor and crisp texture like celery. The edible stalks greatly thickened at their base are also cooked as a vegetable or blanched and eaten like celery. The stalk is a common ingredient in curry powder. I went to the market a few months ago and picked up a finocchio fennel. When I got to the checkout stand the lady asked what it was. I told her and she said she had nothing like that listed. We finally found it under 'anise,' which is unfortunate because the listing in that way refers to another herb entirely.

 ## HISTORY

Fennel first grew in Mediterranean lands, and has been known for so long that it is said to reach as far back as creation. It has been used in the Mediterranean regions for thousands of years in medicine and food. It is now naturalized in the western United States, especially in south and central California and grows wild in Europe and in most temperate countries.

Fennel is found in the records of ancient Egyptians and Greeks. Greeks considered fennel a symbol of success. Greeks of old called fennel "Marathon" as it grew wild surrounding the village of Marathon. The seeds were thought to warm up the metabolism, thus creating weight loss. In Greek mythology, Prometheus concealed the fire of the Sun in a hollow fennel stalk and brought it down to Earth from Heaven for the human race.

Romans believed that serpents sucked the juice of the plant to improve their eyesight, and Pliny recommends the herb for 'dimness of human vision,' and he always declared that the herb enables the 'eye to perceive with clarity the beauty of nature.'

Romans ate the young shoots and fennel was mentioned frequently by the Anglo-Saxons in their cooking and medicinal recipes prior to the Norman Conquest into central Europe. This herb was also cultivated in Charlemagne's imperial farm. In medieval times, chewing the seeds was a favorite way to stop gastric rumbles during church sermons. A broth from the leaves was thought to make fat people thin. In medieval times, bunches of fennel hanging over the door on Midsummer's Eve would prevent witches and other evil spirits from entering. The keyholes were stuffed with seeds as well so ghosts could not enter. The seeds were also used to nibble on during church services in America (the services were very long) because they suppressed the appetite and worked during fasts as well.

In India, fennel seeds are chewed at the end of the meal to soothe digestion and to freshen the breath.

In Elizabethan England, a beverage made from fennel seeds was taken as an antidote for poisonous mushrooms and snakebites.

Fennel was once considered important for disease prevention and is now one of the spices used to flavor certain pizza-type sausage products. Fennel is imported from India, Argentina and Morocco.

 **TYPE** _____

Annual or Florence fennel is grown in cool climates for good 'bulb' formation. The tall and graceful perennial fennel is sometimes cultivated as a biennial. An easy perennial, it can be grown as an annual in colder climates and is hardy to zone 6. Fennel withstands temperatures to about zero degrees. Even if you grow this plant as a perennial, it should be replaced after three years.

DESCRIPTION

My fennel plant dances in the breezes and the six-foot stalks with filigreed leaves look feathery and beautiful. Our bronze plant is in front of our pale green house and surrounded by lovely yellow and white irises; that's enough reason to grow this great herb. Debbie Arenth of Fall City Farms agrees with me and she also loves looking at the lovely fronds. Stems are erect, round, smooth, jointed and branching. Leaves are long and pointed, finely divided green (or bronze), similar to dill foliage. The sweet anise flavor is altogether different from dill.

Tiny yellow flowers are borne on flat umbels in midsummer with 15-40 rays each. The umbels are up to seven inches in diameter. Once the flower umbels have formed, the plant has a new and delightful look to it. By fall, the seed heads contain dozens of half-inch long ribbed seeds that are oval and greenish gray. The seeds are often mistakenly referred to as aniseed because the flavor of the seed resembles that of anise. However, fennel seed is not as strongly aromatic, is larger, and is pale lime-green in color. Fennel seed, derived from the plant of the parsley family, looks very much like cumin and caraway seed. The taproot resembles a carrot.

This tall perennial plant is a familiar sight on wasteland and by the roadside when the yellow flowers are in bloom above a froth of greenery.

PLANTING & CARE REQUIREMENTS

Fennel likes full sun but mine does fine on the eastern side of the house. Common fennel prefers a light, dry, limey soil with pH from 7 to 8.5 and good drainage. It is quite drought tolerant and requires little fertilizer. Seeds are sown in spring directly into the soil as soon as the ground has warmed up. Basically a cool season crop, fennel can be planted early in the year. Plant at a half-inch depth in mid-summer for an early fall harvest. Directly sow seeds in rows eight to twelve inches apart, and thin the plants to 8 inches apart in the row when they reach a few inches in height. The seed should germinate in 14 days. Because the taproot resembles a carrot, it does not like to be moved once planted. Fennel seed may be planted in spring or autumn, but do not sow near caraway or coriander, as they will prevent fennel seeds from forming. Fennel also has a harmful effect on dwarf beans, tomatoes and kohlrabi. Don't plant near dill because cross-pollination will reduce fennel's seed production. When the plants are very young, root rot may occur if over-watered. Aphids may also occasionally infest the plant. Treat with insecticidal soap. Fennel attracts hoverflies, which in turn help keep whiteflies at bay.

Finochccio is grown much like cauliflower and needs a rich, fast-draining soil and lots of moisture to develop the succulent bulb. It grows bulbs of maximum size only in cool weather. In colder climates, start the seed as soon as the soil can be tilled in the spring or plant in mid-summer for a fall harvest. Plant one-half inch deep a few inches apart and keep well watered in the beginning. After germination in 7-10 days, thin to 8 inches apart for full-size bulbs. When the bulb reaches about 1 inch across, draw soil around it to earth up for the remainder of the season as the bulb swells. This is similar to mounding soil around leeks to increase the bulb size. This practice will create not only a larger bulb but a milder flavor as well.

 # HARVESTING

Every part of the fennel plant is edible. You can begin snipping the leaves once the plant is well established. Clippings can be frozen for later use, and as with other herbs, the leaves hold up well when chopped and stored loosely in containers. By clipping the fennel regularly you will keep the plant about one-foot high with thick, robust leaves. Letting it grow at will produces a tall spindly plant that may need to be staked. Leaves and stems should be harvested for fresh use before the plant flowers. Pick flower heads to maintain leaf production if you prefer to not let them go to seed. Harvest seeds the first fall or second summer.

Harvesting the seeds requires precise timing. They will mature about 100 to 115 days after planting. You have to watch the plant closely to notice when the seeds turn from yellowish-green to brown. They will fall to the ground when mature in even a gentle breeze. With scissors, simply snip the entire seed head and let it drop into a paper bag. The roots are edible and may be harvested in the fall of the first year. Cut back old growth in the fall. Fennel will die back into the ground in winter.

It takes approximately 80 days for the stems of Florence fennel to fully mature, but they are edible as soon as they begin to fatten. Just cut them off at the crown. For the plumpest stems, pinch off the emerging seed head and give them several more days. Some say that the stems are at their best when the plant is just about to bloom.

Florence fennel cultivated by market gardeners is found in greengrocers' shops during winter and spring. When buying, cut off some of the copious foliage, leaving two or three fronds and store in the cool compartment of the refrigerator for other uses. To harvest from your garden, cut off the plant at ground level with a sharp knife. Harvest when bulbs are about baseball size. However, in some seasons you may not get this size. When lifting, cut the globe cleanly away from the root system. They may then resprout and produce small usable side shoots much like broccoli or cabbage. The enormous creamy bulbs are usually tied together by their bushy tops in bundles of two or three.

 ## PRESERVATION

When dried, the leaves lose flavor so it's better to use them fresh or to freeze them in small batches in plastic bags. The leaves may also be infused in oil or vinegar.

Seeds have much stronger flavor than the leaf. Once they have dried in the paper bag for two to three weeks, store in a warm, dark place for further drying. You will need to pick out the dried stems to which the seeds were attached.

These are not edible. Once the seeds are thoroughly dried, they can be transferred to jars for year-round keeping. The seeds may also be frozen. Fennel seeds contain anethole, the volatile oil that accounts for their licorice flavor. Pulsing whole seeds in a coffee grinder before use really releases the volatile oils.

 # PROPAGATION

Fennel is nearly always propagated by seed. If you wish lots of plants in the spring it will readily self-seed if the seed heads are left on the plant. This practice, however, might cause fennel plants to propagate throughout the neighborhood because those gentle spring breezes usually turn into windstorms in the fall and winter and can carry the seed a long distance.

As described in the section on Planting & Care Requirements, the seed can be directly sown in the spring after danger of frost has passed or by transplanting. The plants should also be divided every three to four years. These roots make great starter plants for fellow gardeners. Florence fennel is best transplanted once for best bulb production.

 # MEDICINAL USES

All parts of the plant are safe for human consumption. The volatile oil, however, can be irritating or even dangerous to those with allergies or skin sensitivities. Culpeper believed that fennel helped break kidney stones, quieted hiccups, prevented nausea and gout, cleared the liver and lungs, and served as an antidote to poisonous mushrooms. In Chinese medicine, the seeds are thought to be tonifying for the spleen and kidneys, and are used for urinary and reproductive disharmonies. Hippocrates was the first to advocate fennel for treatment of infant colic. Four hundred years later, Dioscorides recommended the seeds to nursing mothers to boost milk production. A weak solution of fennel tea may be given to an uncomfortable baby, with or without milk, to help bring up wind and to soothe the baby. This is also a good woman's herb for PMS, stomach cramps and fatigue. Fennel is a uterine stimulant, so avoid high does of the herb in pregnancy. Small amounts used in cooking are safe. Latin Americans still boil fennel seeds in milk to be ingested as a breast milk promoter by nursing mothers. When a nursing mother takes an infusion of seeds, it can relieve colic in babies. A fennel poultice can relieve swelling in the breasts of nursing mothers.

Fennel was one of nine sacred herbs with the power to cure the nine causes of medieval diseases.

In China it is known as "Hu-xiang"and used as a tonic for the spleen, kidney, and reproductive organs. Jamaicans use it to treat respiratory problems and Africans swear by it for diarrhea and digestive upsets. In fact, while typing this chapter, I am pleasantly imbibing on a teapot of fennel and lemon verbena tea as I have been suffering digestive upset and diarrhea for several days. It is very soothing for digestion and eases heartburn and constipation when used as a tea. It may be given in small quantities to help young children digest carbohydrates.

Fennel is a mild expectorant helping to loosen coughs, congestion and asthma. Drinking tea or simply chewing the seeds also has a reputation for helping weight-reducers to slim as it aids in lowering the appetite. Warm tea can be used as a weak diuretic or for constipation and other urinary disorders.

Extract of the seed is an anti-inflammatory, easing gout, arthritis and rheumatism.

Use to strengthen the eyesight. The belief in fennel's ability to benefit the eyes has persisted through the centuries - it was an old custom to wash the eyes of a newborn baby with fennel water, and herbalists today recommend bathing weakened, sore or inflamed eyes with fennel tea.

Use an infusion as a gargle for gum disorders, loose teeth, laryngitis or sore throats and even as a breath freshener.

Fennel oil extracted from crushed seeds is useful for massage, baths, inhalation, poultices, and compresses.

 OTHER USES _____

Fennel is used in many simple beauty aids. A strong brew of fennel, cooled, then mixed with a teacup of yogurt, a little honey and one tablespoon of Fuller's Earth can be applied as a face pack to rejuvenate the skin. Fennel tea and honey is also a good facial pack for smoothing and erasing wrinkles. A facial steam softens the skin. A lotion can be made to bathe tired eyelids. Fennel vinegar makes a good skin tonic, which cleanses and invigorates the skin with an astringent action. Because this herb is a circulatory stimulant, a few drops of fennel oil in a warm bath will have an energizing effect. An instant pick-me-up can be felt by inhaling a few drops on a tissue, aromatherapy style.

 CULINARY USES _____

Romans valued fennel in their banquets where they ate its leaf, root and seed in salads and baked it in bread and cakes. It was good seasoning for fatty dishes like pork, stuffing, poultry and lamb. This much-in-demand herb has many uses in the kitchen today as well. Fennel is a storehouse of valuable nutrients including vitamin A and potassium. It is also high in calcium, iron, and vitamin C and contains some protein and phosphorus as well.

Heat destroys the delicate flavor of fennel leaves, so add to cooked recipes at the very last moment. The fresh leaves give a wonderfully delicate appearance to most all dishes and the fronds make a pretty presentation when laid across the food on the plate. Its frilly tops in green and bronze are anise-like in flavor, and when chopped are also a great addition to soups and salads. Mince and add to a creamy dressing for fish salads or to creamy fish soups. Chop the fronds and use in red fish stews or cioppino, marinated tomatoes or cucumber salad, or mix them into soft cheeses. Try them over buttered new potatoes. Fennel is excellent with oily fish such as salmon because it helps in digestion. Chop in a blender and add vinegar and olive oil for a wonderful dressing. Add leaves to water for poaching or boiling fish or lobster. I have used fennel with cheese, breads, pastry, pickles, soups and consomme', vegetables of all kinds, and with duck, barley and rice. Fennel seeds in sauerkraut is one of my husband's favorites. You can even use the bright yellow flowers in soups and salads.

Debbie Arenth uses fennel fronds in her organic salad mix along with borage flowers. She also likes bronze fennel on strawberries with sour cream. Now that is one I must try as soon as my fennel plant is growing heartily again.

Seeds of the fennel taste earthy like a combination of licorice, lemon and pine. Whole or ground seeds are used in breads and bakery goods, soups, sauces, marinades and fish dishes. Made into a tea, fennel calms digestive disturbances. The seeds can also be used for their health-giving qualities. Try fennel seeds in place of caraway or dill in potato soup, rye breads and salads and crackers or with sweet pickles and cookies. Add ground seed to hot or chilled tomato soup. The seeds are great in many kinds of desserts and beverages.

Fennel stalks can be added to your barbecue coals or lava rock to impart a wonderful flavor to hamburgers or chicken. Eat stems of Florence fennel raw as celery or in a salad. Boiled, blanched stalks make a wonderful vegetable in and of themselves. The flavor is subdued when cooked and tastes like a nuttier flavor of anise. The young stems add an extra crunch to salads.

Large supermarkets generally have Florence fennel bulbs year around. When selecting a fennel, look for fresh, aromatic foliage, unbruised bulbs, and compact stems.

The swollen stem base of finocchio has a crisp texture and fragrant aniseed flavor, and is excellent when sliced thinly and tossed in French dressing as a salad, or cut in half and cooked as a vegetable. Florence fennel bulbs can be sliced raw in green salads, sautéed, or quartered in chicken casserole. Mince a bulb and add to a salad of avocado and grapefruit. Raw, it has a celery-like crunch; cooked, it is richer and mellower, adding a delicate sweetness to dishes. Anise or licorice flavor goes well with grilled fish, vegetable dips, and cream sauces. After adding all that fiber to your diet for good health, you may be suffering more gas then previously. Just chew a few fennel seeds to settle your discomfort. Thank goodness for fennel.

 RECIPES

To prepare fennel bulb, wash, cut off the bottom and remove the stems and leaves. Discard any tough or bruised outside pieces. Fennel darkens quickly with air contact, so cook it immediately or sprinkle it with citrus juice to preserve its color.

Fennel, Arugula, & Orange Salad

I especially like this combination because fennel is so good with citrus fruits.

⅓ cup walnuts or pine nuts
2 oranges
1 fennel bulb, washed
1 head leafy lettuce (not iceberg)
1 bunch of arugula (1-2 cups)
Fennel leaves for garnish

Place the nuts on a baking sheet and roast for 3-5 minutes at 350° F. Remove from the oven, cool, and set aside. Peel the oranges, removing the rind and white pith. Cut the sections away from the center removing any seeds. Set aside, saving 1 Tbs. of the juice for dressing. Slice the fennel bulb thinly and set aside. Tear the lettuce into pieces and arrange in a large shallow bowl. Scatter the arugula, fennel, and orange slices on the lettuce, and sprinkle nuts on top. Garnish with a few tips of the fennel leaves. Drizzle with dressing made from: 3 Tbs. olive oil, 2 Tbs. light fruity vinegar (raspberry, blueberry, cranberry), 3 Tbs. strong, well-flavored tea such as Earl Gray, 1 Tbs. reserved orange juice, 1 tsp. Dijon-style mustard, salt and pepper to taste. Mix ingredients until well blended and serve.

Fennel or Finocchio Salad
(Serves 2)
Take one large fennel bulb and trim off the stalks, then wash the globe thoroughly. With a knife, slice thinly across, separating the circles like onion rings. Pat dry and place in a wooden bowl with salt, pepper, 2 Tbs. vegetable oil and 1 Tbs. white or cider vinegar. Toss well and serve. A few lettuce leaves or good black olives can be added for variety along with fresh snipped parsley.

Fennel & Tomatoes with Dill
4 small Finochhio fennel roots
Canola oil
1 lb. tomatoes
3 Tbs. chopped dill

Cut the fennel into very thin vertical slices. Heat enough oil to cover the bottom of a heavy pan and stew the fennel gently, stirring often, until almost soft. Add plenty of salt and pepper. Skin and slice the tomatoes. Add them to the fennel and continue to cook gently for 5 minutes, stirring to break up the tomatoes. When ready, stir in the chopped dill and turn into a dish to cool. Serve cold, but do not chill.

Fennel Bulbs with White Sauce
(Serves 4)
2 fennel bulbs
1 cup thick white sauce (See below)
2 Tbs. grated cheese (Parmesan or Pecorino)

Trim the bulbs, wash them and cut each one in half lengthwise. Place in boiling water and simmer about 20 minutes or until tender. Drain, and then lay the cut side down in an ovenproof dish.

Cover with the white sauce and sprinkle on cheese. Place under the broiler or put in a hot oven at 400° F. for a few minutes until the cheese melts and browns a little.

White Sauce: Melt 1 Tbs. butter or margarine in a saucepan over medium heat. Stir in 1 to 2 Tbs. flour, add 8 oz milk, and stir until thick.

Fennel Biscotti

I came up with this, my favorite fennel recipe, when I collected about one quart of fennel seeds last year. I serve it at my herbal luncheons along with the lavender and lemon verbena ice cream found in another chapter. My guests love it and I know you will love it, too.

3 cups flour, sifted
2 ½ tsp. baking powder
1 cup sugar
½ tsp. salt
3 large eggs, beaten
½ cup butter, melted and cooled
2 Tbs. fennel seeds, bruised
2 Tbs. Sambucca liqueur

Grease two baking sheets. Preheat oven to 350° F. In a large mixing bowl, combine flour, baking powder, sugar and salt; set aside. In a separate bowl, combine beaten eggs with melted butter. Place slightly bruised fennel seeds and Sambucca in the microwave on high for 20-30 seconds then add to the egg mixture. Make a well in the center of the flour mixture and stir in the egg mixture. Turn out onto a lightly floured board and knead until smooth. Shape dough into four long rolls, each about as wide as your thumb, and arrange several inches apart on the greased cookie sheets. Bake 20 minutes, or until rolls are golden brown and slightly flattened. Transfer cookie rolls to cooling rack and cool 10 minutes. Slice each roll on a long diagonal into ½-inch slices and return slices to cookie sheets. Bake 10 minutes or until slightly brown, then turn each cookie over and bake 10 minutes longer. Cool cookies on racks and store tightly covered.

Grilled Fish with Fennel

1 whole fish per person (I like trout), cleaned and scaled
Salt and freshly ground pepper
Slices of lemon cut thinly
1 small bunch green or bronze fennel leaves

With a sharp knife make about 4 incisions on one side across the fish diagonally but don't slice through. Dust the uncut side with salt and pepper, and place on the grill with the cut side down. When the cut side is cooked, turn the fish over carefully and press lemon pieces into alternate incisions, then press 2-inch long fennel fronds into the alternate incisions. Season with salt and pepper, place on the grill again and cook until done. If the fish seems dry while cooking, baste with a little olive oil. Cook fish for 8 minutes (4 on each side) for every inch of thickness.

Grilled Salmon with Fennel Butter Sauce

2 lb. skinless, boneless salmon filet
Salt & pepper to taste
2 Tbs. olive oil
1 bulb fennel, about ¾ lb.
⅓ cup water
5 Tbs. butter at room temperature
⅛ tsp. cayenne pepper
⅛ tsp. fresh nutmeg

Remove any bones in the fish. Cut the fillets into four portions and sprinkle with salt and pepper. Sprinkle with oil and rub to coat all sides. Set aside. Trim the fennel and cut into ¼ inch cubes (about 1-½ cups). Put the fennel in a saucepan, add the water and 1 Tbs. of butter and cook 5 minutes. Pour the mixture into the container of a food processor or electric blender and add the remaining butter. Blend as finely as possible. There should be about 1-¼ cups. Pour the mixture into a small saucepan and bring to a boil. Add salt, pepper, cayenne pepper and nutmeg. Let simmer about 3 minutes. Meanwhile, heat a skillet or grill and add the salmon pieces. Cook about 4 minutes on one side. Turn and cook another 4 minutes. Transfer the pieces to a warm serving dish. Serve with the hot fennel sauce spooned over or on the side with a sprig of fresh fennel.

Fennel Stuffing for Fish

1 small onion, peeled and chopped
2 Tbs. butter
1 cup soft, fresh bread crumbs or small bread cubes
Salt and pepper
2 Tbs. chopped fennel leaves
1 egg

Sauté the onion in melted butter until light brown. Remove from the heat and stir in the breadcrumbs. Add salt and pepper to taste, then stir in the chopped fennel. Beat the egg and stir it in. Use to stuff fish before baking or grilling.

Pork Chop Minestrone

This seems like a lot of ingredients and takes some time, but it really is worth it and a meal all by itself.
(Serves 4)

1 cup dried white beans or small limas
Water to cover
1 tsp. fennel seed, crushed
3 cups regular-strength chicken stock
¼ lb. salt pork, diced
1 small onion, quartered
1 large clove garlic, minced
1 8-10 oz can tomatoes
2 med. carrots, peeled and cut in half crosswise
4 small thin-skinned potatoes, scrubbed (each about 1-½ inch across)
1 medium zucchini (ends trimmed) cut crosswise into quarters
4 smoked bone-in pork loin chops cut ½ to ¾ inch thick (1 ½ lb. total)
1 cup lightly packed fresh basil leaves
Salt and pepper
½ cup grated Parmesan cheese

Sort through beans, removing any debris. Rinse beans and combine with 3 cups water in a 2-3 quart pan. Bring to a boil, over high heat; boil 2 minutes. Cover and let stand 12 hours, drain. (Or you can use canned beans, drained). To drained beans, add 3 more cups water, fennel seed, and 1 cup of chicken broth. Bring to a boil on high heat; reduce heat, cover, and simmer until beans mash readily (45 minutes to 1 hour). Ladle half of the beans and ½ cup of the cooking liquid into a food processor or blender; whirl until beans are coarsely pureed (or mash them with a potato masher). Return the beans to the cooking pan; set aside. In a 4-5 quart pan over medium heat, combine salt pork, onion, and garlic; cook, stirring frequently, until onion is browned at edges, about 5 minutes. To pan, add the beans and liquid, remaining 2 cups of chicken broth, tomatoes and their liquid, carrots, and potatoes. Bring to a boil, cover, and simmer 15 minutes. Add the zucchini chunks and pork chops; simmer uncovered until the vegetables are tender when pierced about 10 minutes longer. Meanwhile, chop half of the basil. Add chopped and whole basil leaves and salt and pepper to taste. Gently ladle into wide, shallow soup bowls, dividing pork and vegetables equally. Offer cheese in a small bowl.

Pasta Sauce with Cheese and Fennel
3 Tbs. butter
3 Tbs. flour
2 cups milk
½ cup grated Swiss cheese
½ cup grated Parmesan or Romano cheese
2 Tbs. fresh fennel
1 lb. cooked penne pasta

Melt butter in a saucepan. Add flour, stirring constantly with a whisk. Slowly add the milk and bring just to the boiling point, stirring constantly. Add the two cheeses and stir until well blended. Add fennel and mix together. Toss well with the cooked pasta.

Italian Sausage with Fennel
I like to make my own sausage so that I can control the fat content. This is one of my favorites.

4 lbs. pork shoulder or butt, with most of the fat removed
1 Tbs. coarsely-ground fennel seed
2 bay leaves, crushed finely

3 Tbs. chopped parsley
5 garlic cloves, minced
½ tsp. red pepper flakes
3 Tbs. salt
Pepper to taste
1 cup grated Parmesan or Romano cheese
¾ cup dry red wine, a Cabernet is good
4 yards sausage casings

Grind the meat in a kitchen processor to a coarse texture. Rinse
your hands in warm water and mix all ingredients together and
allow to sit at least one hour before stuffing into casings. Casings
can be purchased from the butcher shop. Tie the casing at 6 inch
intervals in two places, then cut between strings to form individual
sausages. To cook, place in a frying pan with a little bit of olive oil
and just enough water to cover the bottom of the pan. Cover and
cook until the water evaporates. Then, continue to brown, turning
once. Sausages may also be hung and dried for a few hours before
cooking or storing. Of course, you can use this recipe for sausage
patties.

Fennel Tea
Bruise 1 tsp. of fennel seeds in a mortar and pestle; simmer for 5
minutes in a cup of water. Cool and use as a facial steam or as a tea
for indigestion.

Fennel Seed Vinegar
Gently pound or bruise 2 Tbs. fennel seed in a mortar. Add 1 cup
white wine or cider vinegar. Heat another cup of vinegar until
warm but not boiling, and pour a little over the seeds in the mortar.
Pound further to release the flavors of the herb. Mix with
remaining vinegar in a bottle. Seal tightly with a cork. Put on a
sunny windowsill and shake each day for 2-3 weeks. Test for flavor
then strain through muslin and rebottle. Add a fresh fennel sprig
for identification. (Also can combine with dill seeds.)

Fennel vinegar can also be made with fennel fronds, some garlic
and parsley.

Fennel Steam

Herbs cause a deep cleansing of the face and neck areas when skin looks dull with poor color and feels clogged.

4 Tbs. fennel seeds, bruised (crushed)
1 quart water, boiled

Simmer seeds in water for 8 minutes. When cool enough; place face within 10 inches with a towel over your head. Don't burn your skin but try to stay under the towel 5-10 minutes. Use a thin film of oil before steaming if your skin is dry. Pat dry with a soft towel.

Fennel Face Pack

Chopped fennel leaves
Plain yogurt

Mix chopped leaves with the yogurt and spread on face, avoiding the eyes and mouth. Leave on for 15-20 minutes then rinse with warm water. This will act as a tonic for the skin and smooth away wrinkles. Use weekly for best results.

Fennel Eye Bath

Simmer ½ tsp. fennel seed in ½ pint water for three minutes. Strain and cool. Bathe eyes or place soaked cotton balls on eyelids for five minutes. Store in sterile jar and keep refrigerated. Or you may use this bath as a compress on eyelids to ease inflammation or watery, tired eyes.

 OTHER NOTES _____

Fennel oil is sweetly aromatic in both odor and taste. It is used commercially in condiments and hand creams, perfumes, liqueurs, and soaps. Oil of fennel includes 50-60 percent anethol, which is also the chief constituent of anise oil, and 18-22 percent fenchone, a pungent, colorless liquid. Fennel oil is used to relieve external pain of rheumatism, arthritis, and sore muscles, but can cause skin reaction in sensitive people. Fennel is used in a soothing bath.

Fennel makes a mustard-yellow to golden-brown dye when flowers or leaves are used. Fennel is cleansing and medicating. It was believed that snakes ate the plant to restore their sight after shedding their skins, so it became known as a remedy for eye ailments.

Fennel (as well as Lovage) attracts a huge black-and-chartreuse-striped caterpillar, which eventually grows up to be the gorgeous anise swallowtail butterfly. The female lays her eggs on the plant and from each egg a green-and-black-striped caterpillar hatches, grows, pupates and is transformed into a butterfly all the while living and feeding on the fennel plant. The wingspread has patterns of orange, blue, black, lemon and white. The first year I saw these caterpillars on my lovage and fennel plants I removed them and killed them! What did I know? Then I became a Master Gardener and learned of their importance in the garden. Now I let the caterpillars eat their share of the plant and I get the benefits of this beneficial butterfly in my garden. The anise swallowtail and black swallowtail rely on fennel.

Fennel seed is still being used to flavor liqueurs, such as Sambucca. In the Middle Ages, fennel was a favorite strewing herb because of its fragrance and its help in keeping insects at bay. It was used in the kitchen to protect and lend flavor to food, which was often far from fresh. The seed was recommended for obesity, as it dulls appetite.

LEMON VERBENA

The Best Soap On Earth

LEMON VERBENA

I grow lemon balm, lemon gem marigold, lemon thyme and several others, but lemon verbena is my favorite lemon herb. Lemon verbena stands for enchantment or delicacy of feeling in the language of flowers. Although this herb is only occasionally in demand (and not available in any market I have ever seen) when people learn of its excellent qualities, I think more will be growing their own.

 ## BOTANICAL NAME _____

Lemon Verbena – _Aloysia triphylla_ – _(Lippia citriodora_ or _Aloysia citriodora)_ – are old names and has such strongly perfumed leaves that when brushing past the foliage, one is surrounded by a most refreshing light fragrance redolent of lemons. Lemon verbena belongs to the _Verbenaceae_ family. There are over 30 species of lemon verbena throughout the world, but _Aloysia triphylla_ is the most common and most recognized. Lemon verbena is making a resurgence nationally with the interest in many old varieties of herbs. Another verbena, the herb, vervain (_Verbena officinalis_), is found in herbal lore. Vervain in appearance and scent is completely different from Lemon verbena.

 ## HISTORY _____

In the early 1500's, Spanish explorers, chasing wisps of rumor, pushed inland from the Pacific coast of South America questing for "Sweat of the Sun"- gold. On the border of what are now Peru and Chile, they discovered treasure of another sort - a previously unknown plant that charmed them immensely. We know the plant today as Lemon verbena. Ounce for ounce, it's considered by many to be the most pleasantly lemon-scented plant in the world. The history of this bush does not go far back in European records, having been introduced into England from Chile about 1784. This is a rare instance of an herb being introduced from the New World to the Old instead of the other way around.

Lemon verbena is now widely cultivated and grown commercially in France and North Africa where the plants may reach 10-15 feet tall, but because they are so sensitive to cold weather, North Americans usually confine them to containers. The plant has been introduced to various parts of the world and is widely grown in warm, temperate areas of Europe and naturalized in the Mediterranean region where it has escaped from cultivation. In India, it has been a common plant in gardens since it was introduced to that country.

 **TYPE** _____

This sweet-scented tender or half-hardy perennial grows well in our zone 7 and 8 climate as long as we keep it in a pot with the roots well-mulched in winter. It is plant hardy, however, in zones 9-10. Depending on where the plant grows, it can be considered either a tender deciduous shrub or an evergreen.

 **DESCRIPTION** _____

Although a newcomer to the herb garden compared with most herbs, lemon verbena is soon loved by all who know it. Its usual height is 2-5 feet but it can reach 10-15 feet outdoors in warm climates with a spread of up to 8 feet. In our cooler latitudes, grown in a pot, or kept indoors, it rarely reaches over 5 feet. When it does get over 10 feet, it usually gets scraggly looking. I did see a very large lemon verbena in San Diego that must have been at least 15 feet high, but it was not very compact.

This shrub-like plant is encased in crisp, light green leaves on 2-4 foot stalks or stems. The 3-4 inch long leaves have margins toothed and fringed with slightly sticky hairs on them. This deciduous, woody shrub's flowers have a very distinctive lemon fragrance. The tiny, tubular flowers are white tinged with lavender, in spikes with four stamens. The shrub flowers in mid to late summer, July to September, and even the flowers are very tasty. The fruit has two seed-like nutlets enclosed by a calyx.

Although not a terrifically showy plant, new shoots appear on the shrub in spring and become quite thick with foliage by midsummer. The foliage is very attractive in the garden and lends a cheery fragrance. This alone should give it passage to any garden.

 PLANTING & CARE REQUIREMENTS __

Lemon verbena must be grown in a warm, sheltered position - preferably at the base of a south-facing wall. A well-drained, medium rich-to-poor soil with a pH of 6.5 is ideal. Although it will tolerate partial shade, it really prefers full sun. The soil should be kept moist but not soggy since it needs good drainage.

Grow lemon verbena in a container unless you live in the warmer zones 9 or 10. Even in warmer climates, it needs protection against frost, wind and any temperature below 40° F. In severely cold conditions, protect the roots of the bush with mulch, leaf mold or hay. Mulch roots well if left in the ground. These plants can be trained as a standard - a formal shape like that of a lollipop tree.

Because this herb feeds heavily, apply regular applications of fish emulsion. Mist or wash the leaves weekly to keep mites from colonizing. When setting container-grown lemon verbena outdoors, place the pots on a hard surface, such as tile or bricks, to keep the roots from escaping the pots and entering the ground. Potted plants that have rooted will suffer shock if their roots are broken free from the ground; such shock will ultimately shorten the lives of the plants.

Lemon verbena will grow well indoors if you have it in a big pot - you know it really is a large bush or small tree! - and give it lots of sun. Water frequently without letting it become soggy. Feed with liquid fertilizer during flowering. Once buds are evident, remove dead tips and prune gently to encourage new growth.

Spider mites and whiteflies are the worst enemy of lemon verbena and can infest them. Spray infested leaves with a mixture of cold water and insecticidal soap. I have also tried a slurry of flour, buttermilk, and water as an effective spray. Of course, lacewings, ladybugs or predatory mites are organic ways to protect your plants. The lacewings will stay around even after they have eaten all the mites, but ladybugs, as the old saying goes, fly away, fly away home. Yellow sticky traps are available from nurseries and work much like flypaper. This is most effective if you have your plant in a greenhouse or indoors. I also have had some luck using Feverfew, a perennial flower - it really smells nasty! Soak a handful of fresh Feverfew leaves in a quart of boiling water for one hour, then strain and use as a garden spray.

Sometimes the plant does not start producing leaves until summer. Don't assume it's dead until late spring. Then cut into the wood to see if it is white, green or brown; if it is brown and breaks easily, the plant is probably a goner.

If shrubs are planted directly in the garden, they can be cut back to the ground in late fall if the temperature falls below 20° F. Dig up the roots and 'heel' them in moist sand in a cellar or basement. Water the roots every few weeks to keep them from drying out. Once danger of frost has passed the following spring, replant the roots. If you use this method, the plants should grow up to four feet high each year. They can also be potted up and brought into the house or garage for the colder months. The change in climate, however, will usually cause the leaves to drop. (See the Preservation section.)

 **HARVESTING**

Both the leaves and flowers of lemon verbena can be harvested either fresh or after they dry. Pinch tips of the plant to keep it bushy. If you bring the plant inside as described above, leaves will shed in winter with the change of climate. Simply set the plant on layers of newspaper and leaves will dry by themselves and drop to the paper.

The plant should be pruned back in early spring. After trimming established plants in spring, spray with warm water to help them revive. If your plant has been outdoors during the summer, cut away the very thin branches before bringing it in for the winter. Thin branches will become weak and straggly and detract from the appearance and vigor of the plant. These discards, however, will effuse a delightful fragrance, so place them in a dresser drawer to scent your clothes or in a closet. Cut the plant back halfway in midsummer and again before the first frost. Bring it indoors before frost.

Don't be concerned when your lemon verbena loses its leaves in the fall. At other times of year, however, leaf loss is a sign that plants are under stress, perhaps caused by lack of water or root shock. If this occurs, hold back on watering for a little while. Lack of leaves reduces transpiration, and the plant will not be able to handle large quantities of water. Keep your lemon verbena on the dry side until it starts perking up again. Then return to your normal watering routine. You can also harvest sprigs of leaves all year long and the flowers when they are in bloom. If you grow lemon verbena in warmer climates and don't want your plant to get 10 feet tall, you can trim it weekly to keep it shorter.

PRESERVATION _____

The purpose of drying herbs is to eliminate the water content of the plant quickly and, at the same time, to retain the essential oil. The faster the drying time (as long as the temperature is not too high) the better the retention of aromatic essential oil. Darkness helps prevent loss of color and unique flavors. Good air circulation will hasten drying and discourage mold. Lemon verbena dries particularly well.

One unique way to preserve some lemon verbena is to gather an armful of leafy and flowering branches before midday and stack them at the back of a linen cupboard so the leaves as they dry perfume your linens.

The leaves need to be dried in a warm, dark and well-ventilated place. Do not hang them in the kitchen, as there is too much light. You may let them dry on the plant and then fall onto newspaper, or you may remove the leaves and dry them in a dehydrator or in an oven turned on low with the door ajar. You can hang leaves and stems in bunches in a dark place, but you need to place a brown paper bag with holes in it over them to catch the leaves.

Leaves should be brittle and crisp when completely dry. Keep the leaves as whole as possible to preserve the volatile oil. No matter which method you use, the leaves usually dry quickly with no mold or mildew problems. After drying, carefully remove the leaves and store in an airtight container. When using the dried leaves, first rub them between your fingers or crush them in the palm of your hand to release the wonderfully rich lemony volatile oil. Dried lemon verbena keeps its scent for many months.

PROPAGATION _____

Lemon verbena is usually propagated by cuttings. They can also be grown from seed, but the plant produces few seeds. Softwood cuttings can be taken in the middle-to-late-summer. Always take cuttings from a strong pest-and-disease free plant that has been watered and fed sufficiently to produce an abundance of cuttings. Taking cuttings often causes the plant to wilt, so it's best to keep the donor in the shade and make sure it is well watered. The best cuttings are taken from stems of one-fourth inch in diameter or smaller on green wood. Cut below a leaf joint and use a sharp, clean knife. Take a cutting six inches long leaving two leaf joints, one with leaves above the rooting medium, the other below. Strip off the bottom leaves, dip the cutting in hormone powder, and insert it into a container. Three leaves should be left on the upper joint. Cut the outer half of each leaf off. These cuttings wilt quickly, so be prepared to immediately mist. Fill a container with seed compost, firm it at the base, then fill loosely leaving no air pockets. Compost should be moist, not wet. Label the container with the name of the plant and date, then place it on a propagation mat, or heated bed, and water. Roots will develop according to the time of the year. Lift and inspect the containers from time to time; when roots begin to show through the compost, remove them from the heated bed. Wean them by giving less water for a few days before potting them up. Keep the cuttings in pots for the first two years.

Late summer or early autumn semi-hardwood cuttings can be taken and treated the same way as the above softwood cuttings. Whenever you take cuttings, be sure the plant is in a productive growing cycle.

MEDICINAL USES

This is not an important medicinal herb, probably because of its late introduction to Europe. Lemon verbena is used in folk medicine in Latin America for colds, colic, diarrhea, fever, and dyspepsia. It's used in treating colds and fever in North Africa as well. Drink a tea of lemon verbena after a heavy meal to settle digestion, or to make a lovely dessert!

The volatile oil in lemon verbena is antispasmodic and reportedly produces a tonic effect on the stomach and intestines. The tea is a real stress reliever as well as aiding depression, nervous stomachs and headaches. At night it's a natural way to help sleep in its role as a sedative.

Using the branches fresh or dried in tisanes for reducing fevers, or to reduce heart palpitations can preserve the antibacterial activity of the volatile oil. It makes an excellent cooling tea in very hot weather, either on its own or added to other tea ingredients.

Infused lemon verbena used in cleaning the teeth by simply swishing the liquid in the mouth is good for gums and helps prevent tooth decay

 # OTHER USES

I use lemon verbena in my garden to attract the neighborhood children. I love children and teaching them about the attributes of herbs. Little Miles Rich sampled my lemon verbena tea with lavender sugar and proclaimed it was "yummy." This was a reaction from a child who is very reticent to try anything new. While sipping our tea on a very cold winter's day, we examined the first flowers in the garden where the winter snowdrops and the early blooming camellias were budding. After seeing the sticks left on the lemon verbena plant during the winter, Miles exclaimed, "It looks like a scarecrow that the crows ate." I have to admit the plant is not too attractive at that time.

The essence of the volatile oil makes lovely bars of fine soap. (See the soap recipe below.) One of the main uses for dried lemon verbena leaves is in potpourri or sachets, lending a light, piercing scent in contrast to sweet and spicy perfumes. Bath salts, cleaning teeth and gums, skin cleansers and sleep pillows are also popular uses. Add a sprig to a tussie-mussie or a bouquet of flowers. Place leaves in finger bowls instead of slices of lemon. The oil is extracted and used to make cologne and toilet water. A simple infusion will work for bath waters. I keep a few fresh leaves in a pocket and take them out to smell frequently to keep my spirits up - its like instant aromatherapy!

By simply brushing the plant, you release its sweet, lemony fragrance. This plant is just a small reminder of the treasures God has so freely given.

 **CULINARY USES** _____

As I continue to grow my one lemon verbena plant over the years, I find more and more uses for its intense citrus taste. The taste of lemon zest without any bitterness is really a bonus in the kitchen. It's the lemoniest of all lemon-scented herbs. When people smell it in my garden, they always go, "wow!"

Listed below is a myriad of ideas on how you can use lemon verbena in the kitchen. Try vinegar with lemon thyme and lemon verbena together (see one of my vinegar recipes). This lemon flavor is wonderful just sprinkled over fresh fruit. Make herbal vinegar using Champagne vinegar with lemon balm, lemon verbena, lemon thyme, lemongrass, and grated lemon zest. I recently decanted a gallon of lemon verbena and red raspberry vinegar that I had mellowing for a few weeks. You might wish to try just rubbing a leaf on a cantaloupe slice. Minced fresh lemon verbena is wonderful in fruit salads, especially with strawberries or blueberries. Add a sprig to homemade jellies or ice cream or line the bottom on a custard dish with lemon verbena before adding the custard. A cake pan can also be lined with the leaves for a pleasant fragrance. To cut down on fat and/or sugar, replace water in dessert recipes with lemon verbena tea.

A delicately flavored tea is a real pick-me-up on dreary days. This lemon-scented and flavored tea can also be served iced on a warm summer day. It's also lovely in most summertime drinks and in a punch in winter. It mixes well with most other tea herbs. The leaves enhance all drinks. Try a combination with mint or anise hyssop. I use the dried leaves in winter and the fresh leaves and flowers for summer. Fresh verbena flowers are used in herbal butters and atop fresh salads.

Finely minced, the leaves are used to flavor fish marinades or steamed with clams and mussels or even added to chicken soup. Add dried, finely-crumbled leaves to the batter when baking carrot, banana, or zucchini bread. To give plain rice a personality, add minced lemon verbena leaves to cooked rice just before serving. In green salads, sauces, soups, or meat dishes and desserts, which call for lemon as an ingredient or a garnish, use lemon verbena instead. Fresh lemon verbena leaves are tough, so unless they are finely minced, be sure to remove them from marinades, beverages, and salad dressings before serving. Heating fresh verbena too much dissipates the flavor so for lighter-flavored cooking, use the dried leaf.

 **RECIPES** _____

I have developed all of these recipes in my kitchen after years of growing lemon verbena. I hope you will try some.

Herb Butter
½ cup sweet cream butter, unsalted
Lemon verbena leaves and/or flowers
Zest from one lemon

Soften the butter and mix in the zest and leaves/flowers with the back of a spoon. Refrigerate in various shapes or freeze for later use.

Lemon Vinegar
(See Tarragon chapter, but substitute)
Lemon verbena leaves
Lemon thyme leaves
Lemon basil leaves
Zest from one lemon
Rice wine vinegar

Lemon Oil
Lemon verbena leaves & flowers
Lemon thyme leaves & flowers
Walnut oil

Warm the oil slightly and crush the leaves and flowers and place in warm oil. Leave to mellow about two weeks. Refrigerate.

Lemon Verbena Tea
Put 20 dried, freshly crushed verbena leaves into a warmed teapot; pour 16 oz boiling water into the pot and cover. Infuse for a few minutes, then strain. Drink hot but without milk, sweetened with honey.

Lemon Verbena Iced Tea
4 Tbs. fresh verbena
4 Tbs. mint leaves (apple or orange)
1 quart of freshly boiled water

Tear the leaves and place in clean, warmed teapot. Add boiling water (never boil the leaves) and let steep, covered, for 10 minutes. Cool completely then pour over ice in glasses. You may also add regular, green, black or oolong tea bags to the teapot first.

Lemon Verbena Bread
1 cup sugar (recipe follows)
½ cup unsalted butter
¼ cup chopped lemon verbena leaves
1 ½ cups sifted flour
1 tsp. baking powder
Pinch of salt
2 large eggs
½ cup milk
Grated zest of one lemon
¼ cup nuts

Cream butter and verbena leaves in a mixer and then add sugar and eggs; beat well and add the remaining ingredients. Pour batter into a buttered 9-inch by 5-inch loaf pan and bake at 350° F. for about 40 minutes. Test to see if toothpick comes out clean. Let the bread cool in the pan. To serve, arrange verbena leaves and flowers on top of the bread.

Lemon Verbena Sugar
2 cups sugar
1 ½ cup fresh lemon verbena leaves

In a jar, layer the sugar and leaves. Shake the jar and leave it on the counter for two to three weeks. When the sugar is completely infused, run it through the processor to mix very well and break down the leaves. (Alternately, you may remove the leaves at this point.) Place the sugar on a cookie sheet or on a Teflon™ sheet in a dehydrator. Dry thoroughly. Run through a processor a final time and bottle. This seems like a lot of work, but I do several kinds of sugar at once so I don't have to wash my processor so much.

Lemon Verbena Rice Pudding
1 ½ cups brown rice
1 Tbs. raw sugar
1 pint milk
8 fresh lemon verbena leaves

Stir the rice, sugar and milk together in a buttered ovenproof dish and lay the verbena leaves on top. Place the dish on the middle shelf of a 350° F. oven and bake 2 to 2 ½ hr. During cooking, stir the pudding gently once or twice with a spoon, sliding the spoon under the skin from the edge. Serve hot or cold with cream or yogurt or with stewed fruit over the top.

Apple Crisp with Lemon Verbena
1 cup rolled oats
2 pounds cooking apples, peeled, cored, and thinly sliced
Juice from 1 lemon
½ cup all-fruit apple butter
2 Tbs. all-purpose flour
⅓ cup dried lemon verbena leaves
2 Tbs. pure maple syrup

Toast the oats in a dry sauté pan over high heat, stirring frequently with a spatula. After about 3 minutes, start watching them carefully, making sure they don't burn. When they're light brown, tip them out of the pan into a bowl and set aside. Combine the apples, lemon juice, apple butter, and flour in a deep 9-inch glass dish. Crumble the lemon verbena between your hands and mix it in. Pour the maple syrup into the oats, stirring so that all the oats are very lightly coated. Scoop the oats over the apple mixture and even out the top. Cover the dish with foil and bake in the center of a 325° F. oven for about 20 minutes or until the apple mixture has begun to bubble. Remove the foil and continue to bake another 5 minutes just until the oats are crisp. Serve warm.

Lemon Verbena/Lavender Ice Cream with Candied Ginger

This recipe seems like a lot of work, and it does take some time, but the lovely delicate flavor is really worth it. I serve it with the fennel biscotti cookies.

2 cups milk
2 cups whipping cream
3 sprigs fresh lavender blossoms
12 fresh lemon verbena leaves
⅓ cup honey or lemon verbena honey
2 Tbs. candied ginger, grated (available in markets)
4 large egg yolks

In a medium saucepan, combine milk, cream, lavender, and verbena. Bring just to a simmer over medium-high heat, stirring constantly. Immediately remove from heat, cover, and let steep 20-30 minutes. Remove and discard the herbs. Stir in honey and ginger; set aside. In a medium bowl, whisk egg yolks until they are very well blended and light yellow. While whisking, slowly pour in about half of the milk mixture. Now, while whisking the remaining milk in the saucepan, slowly add the yolk mixture. Place over medium heat and stir constantly until the mixture thickens enough to coat the back of a spoon - do not let the mixture boil or it will get lumpy. Pour into a large bowl or cold ice cream maker. Refrigerate to cool well. Freeze in the ice cream machine according to directions.

Honey with Lemon Verbena

¼ cup fresh lemon verbena leaves
¼ cup fresh lemon balm or lemon thyme leaves
1 cup fresh catnip leaves and flowers
1 pound dark wildflower honey

Combine the three herbs in a blender or food processor and whiz until very fine. Heat the honey in a small saucepan over medium heat until liquid, then stir in the herbs. Let the mixture cool slightly, then pour in a jar and cover. I leave the herbs in my honey, but others, after mellowing the honey for two weeks, reheat and strain the herb out. I found this a big bother and really like the floating herbs.

Lemon Verbena Sweet Jelly

2 lb. cooking apples, roughly chopped (use cores and peels in place
of bottled pectin)
Large bunch of lemon verbena
2 cups sugar
1 cup water
4 Tbs. chopped lemon verbena

Put the apples into a large pan with the bunch of herbs and cover
with cold water. Bring to a boil and simmer until the apples are soft
(about 30 minutes). Pour into a jelly bag and drain into a bowl
overnight. Measure the strained juice and add 1 lb. sugar to every
1-pint of fluid. Stir over gentle heat until the sugar has dissolved.
Bring to a boil, stirring and boiling until jelly point is reached,
about 20-30 minutes. Dip in a large spoon; tilt spoon until syrup
runs over side. When jellying stage is reached, liquid will stop
flowing in a stream and divide in two distinct drops that run
together and leave the edge of the spoon on one large flake or
sheet. Skim the surface scum and stir in the water and chopped
herb. Pour into jars, seal and label before storing.

Lemon Verbena Soap

Petroleum jelly for soap mold
1 bar soap (Ivory or Castile and glycerin) 1 ¼ cup, grated
1 Tbs. infused lemon verbena water

Water: Add 2 Tbs. of fresh picked and chopped verbena leaves to
½ cup boiling water. Turn to simmer, cover and let simmer 10-15
minutes or until water is reduced by two-thirds. Let cool remaining
covered. Remove the leaves and use one tablespoon for the
infusion.

Soap: Lightly grease the inside of soap molds (any small container
will do). Place soap and water into the top of a double boiler and
heat gently over medium heat. Stir occasionally until all the soap is
melted and resembles a smooth, fluffy white pudding - about 30
minutes. Do not allow the mixture to boil. When all the soap is
melted, carefully spoon it into your prepared molds. Tap the edges
to remove any air bubbles. Place one fresh lemon verbena leaf on

top of each soap, pressing down just a little. Allow to set until soap is cool. Remove from molds and place on wire racks. Let it set for at least 24 hours to breathe then wrap loosely in colorful paper.

 ## OTHER NOTES

In <u>Gone with the Wind</u>, lemon verbena is mentioned as the favorite fragrance of Scarlet O'Hara's mother.

Using a handful each of dried and crumbled lemon verbena, tansy, Southernwood and rosemary, you can make anti-moth herb bags. Mix with one tablespoon whole cloves and a piece of cinnamon stick. Sew into muslin bags and put into drawers and cupboards, or loop the bags onto coat hangers.

For the bath, the delicate lemony aroma works well by itself as a body scent and is an aroma that people seem to find intimate. Try it in a spa for two. Place a handful of fresh or dried leaves in the foot of old pantyhose. The leaves are used as an after-bath body rub and the scent naturally finds its way into commercial soaps and bath oils.

Lemon Verbena can be used as a houseplant. This plant is a favorite garden ornamental as well as providing a popular ingredient in liqueurs.

NOTES

LOVAGE

The Garden's Giant Celery

LOVAGE

Lovage is considered a pot herb especially for spring. Pot herbs are so called because the leaves, and sometimes the roots, of certain plants went into nourishing broths and were also used as cooked vegetables, as well as having their place, raw, in salads. These pot herbs, growing wild along hedgerows, in fields and in woods, were also cultivated in early gardens, especially in monastery gardens, said to be forerunners of today's kitchen gardens. In those early days, it was considered necessary to cleanse the blood after a winter diet of warming, heavy food needed for cold weather. Lovage was used as such a cleanser. This herb is little known and therefore little in demand by consumers.

 ## BOTANICAL NAME

Lovage – _Levisticum officinale_ – is the true lovage but was originally called _Ligusticum levisticum_ and several other botanical names over the years including Italian lovage. The taste is similar to celery, and it has medicinal powers as well. From the _Umbelliferae_ family it is easier to grow than celery. Osha is a species related to common lovage and Chinese lovage is a cousin to garden lovage, but these are not of the same genus and species. There is only one species of lovage. The old name likely came from the Latin word, _ligusticum_, after _Liguria_ in Italy where the herb grew profusely.

 ## HISTORY

Over the centuries, lovage has fallen from fashion. It enjoyed greater popularity in the Middle Ages, when it was grown in kitchen and physic gardens. Even the emperor Charlemagne included the herb in his landscape. The leaves were used in the shoes of travelers during the Middle Ages because lovage is both deodorizing and antiseptic. It helped to revive weary feet - no odor-eaters then!

The Greeks and Romans grew lovage for both its culinary and medicinal uses. In Medieval times the plant was regularly grown in monastery gardens.

Lovage was originally from the Mediterranean region in southern Europe but now is naturalized in much of North America, throughout the temperate regions of the world, and in Australia and Scandinavia. One of the lesser-known herbs today, it was formerly employed a great deal in medicine and cooking, especially in the fourteenth century when it was grown as a drug plant. Among its components are a volatile oil and resins.

TYPE

This large vigorous plant is a stout and hardy perennial. It is hardy to zone 3 and is one of the first herbs to return in the spring. The herbaceous lovage dies back to the ground each winter, but returns bigger and stronger the following summer.

DESCRIPTION

The lovage plant is comparatively large and dramatic for an herb. Vigorous and handsome garden specimens grow from three to six feet tall with a spread of three feet. The stalk can grow to over 10 feet high and has a strong yeasty taste. It dies down in winter.

Stems are smooth, hollow and ribbed like those of celery, erect, thick and more than two feet long. The leaves are darkish green, deeply divided, and large-toothed, broad, flat and wedge-shaped. They are opposite each other on the stem and decrease in size toward the top. The leaves taste rather like both celery and parsley but more strongly of celery. This generally is an acquired taste and my husband still has not acquired it! But I love it.

Tiny, pale, greenish yellow flowers are visible in the summer, generally June and July. These one-and-one-half to four inch oblong-shaped fruit of deep brown seeds follows the flower clusters. The seed is one-fourth inch long, grooved and quite aromatic. The rhizome or root is vertical and strongly aromatic, white, and fleshy, two to three inches thick with branched rootlets up to eight inches long.

 ## PLANTING & CARE REQUIREMENTS___

Lovage does well in almost any garden soil, but performs best in well-drained, rich, moist soil in a sunny or semi-shady location. A pH range of 5.5 to 7.5 is ideal. If you avoid a heavy clay soil with poor drainage, your lovage will grow well and be happy and it will require little care. It will reach full size in three to five years. A hefty application of manure or compost will stimulate heavy leaf production and top growth. The plant will not require mulching if your soil drains well, but keep it well watered during dry spells. After four years, growth tapers off, and the plants simply hold their own for many years to come. This is a great plant for a child's garden because it grows fast-and sometimes taller than they are! If the leaves turn pale, it needs nutrients; if the stems begin to lean over, the plant needs to be cut back or staked.

After cutting back, give the plant fertilizer and it will shoot with new growth. This new young growth is perfect for cooking. To keep it looking good, keep it well clipped. If you let it flower, it will need a support as the flower stalks can grow to 10 feet or more. Lovage will need a period of dormancy during the winter months to complete its growth cycle.

The seeds are only viable for a short time so they should be planted soon after they ripen. Sow the seed in spring or autumn in a seed-box or where the plants are to stay. They may germinate in about 10 days but can take up to four weeks. As the seedlings emerge in the spring they can be transplanted when about three inches high. Fall-planted seed may not germinate until the following spring.

Aphids can be a problem on lovage seeds, so spray with an insecticidal soap such as Safer™. Lovage, like celery, is susceptible to leaf miner. The maggot feeds between upper and lower leaf surfaces, causing white tunnels or blotches on leaves. Watch out for the first tunnels, pick off the affected leaves and destroy them; otherwise, broad dry patches will develop and the leaves will start to wither away. If blotches are severe, cut the plant right down to the ground, burn or destroy the affected shoots. Cover plants with screening or a row cover to prevent infestations.

Lovage is fine grown outside in a large container. Even though it is quite large when planted out in the garden, it can be used in pots where the root system will be restricted by the pot dimensions and by other competing roots if planted with other herbs. It may remain in the same spot as long as it is healthy and productive.

 HARVESTING _____

All parts of this plant may be harvested for a myriad of uses. Once lovage is established, the leaves stems, and roots can be harvested whenever you need them. If you want to encourage bushy growth, clip off the flowers as they appear. Cut the young leaves and stalks frequently. Clip established plants to encourage new shoots in summer. Cut leaves around the edges of the clump to keep the leaves young and producing new shoots. Mature leaves tend to be yellow and bland tasting. After the plant has flowered, the leaves tend to have more of a bitter taste, so harvest in early summer. Stalks or stems of the plant can be cut any time they are mature and used to make candied lovage stems - much like candied angelica stems. (See Recipe section.)

Harvest seed heads when the seeds start to turn brown. Gather and pick the seeds on a dry day when the tiny fruits begin to pop open, indicating they are ripe. Wait two years before harvesting the roots or stems. The roots are surprisingly large, very aromatic and tasty.

PRESERVATION

Remove unblemished leaves from the stems (harvested in the second or third year) before the plant blooms. The leaves may be placed in a single layer on a dehydrator rack or in a very low-heat oven to dry. On a warm day, a rack with good circulation may be placed in the shade with a cover to keep insects away because light will quickly yellow this herb. Stems with leaves attached may be cut and hung in bunches to dry in a shady place. When it is dry, carefully place the brittle, whole foliage into airtight containers.

For drying seeds to use later in baked goods or liqueurs, cut the stems and tie a paper bag over plant heads, and hang upside down in a dry, airy place. Dried stems are hard to find commercially but they do have many uses when rehydrated. The root may be dug for drying in the autumn of the second or third season. To preserve the roots, dig them in the late fall. Wash them, slice into one-half inch pieces and dry them on a screen in a warm, shady place. They can also be dried whole or grated and left in the sun, but at temperatures lower than 125° F. It's not likely to ever reach that heat in our area (even in the sun) but I still prefer my dehydrator where I can control the temperature.

Some people prefer to freeze lovage leaves. Lovage stores fairly well in the freezer. Blanch small bundles of leaves by quickly dunking in boiling water, and then plunging them into an ice bath for two minutes. Drain very well and dry, seal in plastic containers and freeze. The thawed herb will be a bit droopier and softer than when fresh but will still prove satisfactory for cooking. For adding to soups and stews, chop the blanched herb and freeze in ice cube trays much like dill. Take care to thaw only the portion you need because the rest will thaw very quickly and cannot be refrozen.

PROPAGATION _____

New lovage plants can be obtained by direct seeding of fresh seed or by division. Seeds of the lovage plant tend to be moist in the center. These seeds are short lived and will dry out over time. Cold storage in the refrigerator will preserve seeds longer for planting. In this way, you can hold the seeds and then plant them in the late spring. Summer seeding would take place from newly-dropped viable seed to begin a late fall crop.

Alternatively, roots may be divided in spring. Dig the plant when the first reddish leaves emerge from the crown. Don't wait for stalks to appear. Divide the roots with each one having an eye. Replant about two inches deep and two feet apart.

Usually one lovage plant is sufficient, so to procure a plant you might wish to purchase a seedling from a nursery or ask a friend for a start.

MEDICINAL USES _____

There certainly have been a dichotomy of uses of this herb. You will see in the following paragraphs that lovage is supposed to do opposite things in the body, i.e., encourage the appetite but cause weight loss. Just remember most of these 'remedies' have not been scientifically proven, but used for many years. Lovage is an herb that historically has been used more for medicinal than culinary uses. The root is the key ingredient to most of these cures. Taken in one form or another, lovage roots have a diuretic effect and can relieve colic, stomach problems, and obesity. The essential oil is similar to that of angelica. This may explain why lovage is often effective against flatulence. The aromatic root is also a stimulant and carminative. Simply chewing on a bit of the dried root can keep one alert.

Also reported to have sedative action, roots and seeds promote sweating, a warming digestive tonic, and an expectorant for reducing phlegm. An infusion of the root is considered beneficial in many illnesses, including jaundice and urinary troubles.

Externally, preparations of roots or leaves have traditionally been used on boils, for menstrual problems, bladder ailments, cramps, stomach ache, eczema, gout, insomnia, lumbago, sciatica, toothache, and worms. Pregnant women should avoid lovage tea as it can encourage menstruation. Because it is also very effective at reducing water retention, people who are pregnant or who have kidney problems should not take this herb medicinally.

A decoction of the seeds is recommended as a gargle for infections of the mouth and throat, as a drink for pleurisy, and as a wash for bathing sore eyes. Broth made from the seeds or leaves make a diuretic stimulant as well as reducing the appetite and fever. Greeks chewed the seeds to relieve indigestion and flatulence. Some Europeans use it as a folk cure for minor stomach ache, kidney problems, and headaches.

The leaves eaten raw in a salad, or infused as a tea, are recognized as being stimulating for the digestive organs and helpful in remedying gynecological disturbances. Since this herb is an aromatic stimulate, it can be used chopped in special diets as a substitute for hot spices.

This herb is similar to the Chinese herb, *Angelica sinesis* or *dong-qui*, which is also used as *osha ligusticum porterii* by the Pueblo Indians.

 OTHER USES _____

Because of its deodorizing effect, try stuffing lovage leaves into wet, smelly sneakers. The pretty leaves on the stalks make a good background in a floral arrangement. However, this celery-like aroma perfumes your house and may just make you hungry!

Leaves or roots added to the bath water relieves itchy or irritated skin. The leaves are also excellent in bath bags, which can be dried and used repeatedly.

We know that lovage does make a dandy deodorizing herb. A bath like this will not only deodorize, but also will aid in arthritis and rheumatism pain. I have tried it after a day of gardening and it really helps muscle fatigue either as a bath bag, wash cloth or over the showerhead.

Grown as a large container plant on the terrace or patio, lovage makes a great conversation piece for guests. Essence of lovage oil from the root is used in perfumery and in fragrant soaps and creams. It is even used as a flavoring agent for tobacco products and liqueurs and cordials. An infusion made from the seeds was used to erase freckles.

 **CULINARY USES** _____

Lovage leaves, stems, and seeds all taste similar to celery but are much stronger in flavor. Their yeasty taste will be more pleasant if you chop the tender leaves. Use half as much lovage as you would celery.

The new growth has been used in spring tonics for centuries to help wake up the system from heavy dishes eaten all winter. The chopped leaves make a healthful addition to salads, potato and poultry dishes, soup, stews, and some sauces. Try lovage in vinaigrette without salt. Chopped leaves also make a wonderfully tasty addition to carrots, cabbage, and in tomato dishes. It's also great with chicken, poultry stuffing, rice, creamed soups, savory pies, steamed vegetables, and omelets.

The hollow stalks or stems are often preserved as a confection similar to angelica and used to decorate pies and pastry. The root of the plant, like the stem, can also be candied.

Scrape or peel the stems, then blanch them to use in broth, chicken salad, gravy and casseroles. Young stems can be cooked on their own as a vegetable when placed into lightly salted boiling water; simmer until tender and serve with a white sauce. Blanch and marinate lovage stems and serve as a first course, as you would asparagus or leeks. Create a garnish from a lovage stem. Start with a three-inch piece and cut thin slices in it in a spiral effect leaving one and one half inches of stalk. Keep rolling the stem around as you're slicing to make sure all sides are cut. Toss the stem into ice water until the slices curl. Stems can also be puréed or used like celery stalks with dips and mustards.

Crushed seed has a much stronger flavor than either leaves or stems. Use crushed or ground seeds like celery seed for winter soups, in pickling brines, cheese spreads, salads, dressings and sauce. The seed has a particularly well-rounded flavor that adds life to many low-salt or no-salt recipes. Each August, the neighborhood children come over and we cut down the tall, hollow lovage stem, leaving most of the bushy plant to continue growing. We cut the hollow stem into lengths of 6-8 inches each. We then proceed to the vegetable patch and collect ingredients for the Bloody Carol recipe below. Then we sip it through our lovage straws. We've been doing this for years and it has become a late summer tradition. There are lots of things you can do to entertain children in the herb garden!

 **RECIPES** _____

Bloody Carol with Lovage Straws
8 lb. firm tomatoes, washed with stems removed
½ cup chopped lovage
½ cup chopped onion, a mild variety
¼ cup fresh lemon juice
1 Tbs. sugar
2 tsp. salt
2 tsp. Worcestershire sauce
Few drops Tabasco sauce
Lovage straws, 6-8 inches long

Cut tomatoes into pieces and place in an 8-10 quart kettle along with the lovage and onion. Bring slowly to boil, stirring constantly but gently. Cover and simmer about 15 minutes or until soft; stir often to prevent sticking. Press mixture through a food mill or sieve to extract juice and measure 12 cups of juice. Return juice to the kettle and bring to boiling, boil gently, uncovered, about 15 minutes, stirring often to prevent sticking. Measure the remaining juice (you will have about 10 cups) and stir in lemon juice, sugar, salt and sauces. Simmer 10 minutes and cool thoroughly. Serve in glasses with lovage straws. This is lots of fun for kids ages five and older.

Candied Lovage Stems
Green lovage stems (new growth is the tenderest)
Enough water to cover
Sugar equal to water measurement

Cut stems into 3 to 4-inch pieces and blanch (simmer) for two minutes in water; then cool. Peel the stems. Simmer for 20 minutes in syrup made from the equal parts of water and sugar. Drain and reserve the syrup. Refrigerate the stems and syrup separately. Refrigerate for up to 4 days. Reheat the lovage in the syrup and simmer for 20 minutes until candied. The temperature of the syrup should reach 238° F. Drain the lovage and dry on racks set over waxed paper to catch the drips. When dry, store in airtight container and use as a first course or as a decoration on pies, cakes or other pastries.

Vinegar
Lovage seeds, crushed
2 cloves garlic, peeled
Lovage leaves
See the dill recipe section for instructions.

Chicken Stock with Lovage

1 ½ lb. chicken backs, necks, wings
1 large onion, halved
1 large carrot, scraped and halved
1 leek, thoroughly cleaned
1 bay leaf
3 stalks parsley
3 sprigs lovage
Black peppercorns

Rinse chicken pieces; put in large pot and cover with cold water.
Bring to a boil. Drain chicken and remove scum under running
water. Return chicken to the pot and add the onion (with skin on)
and the remaining ingredients. Cover with cold water and bring
to a boil. Lower heat and simmer for about 2 hours. Cool slightly,
strain out the solids and leave just the broth to chill. Chicken fat
will rise to the top and can be removed. If freezing the broth, place
in containers and let fat "seal" in the stock; remove when you use
the broth. I never add salt at the time I make the stock, add it to
your recipe later. If you have the time, you might want to save the
chicken by plucking it from the bone to make chicken noodle soup.

Lovage Soup

This soup makes a great first course to a dinner.

1 oz. butter or margarine
2 Tbs. flour
2 cups chicken stock
5 oz. milk
1 Tbs. chopped lovage leaves
2 tsp. lemon juice
Salt to taste

Melt the butter in a saucepan; add the flour and blend to a smooth
paste. Gradually pour in the stock, heat and stir until thickened.
Add the milk, lovage and lemon juice. Simmer for 15 minutes. Add
salt to taste. Put through a sieve or purée in a blender. Serve hot or
cold, garnishing each serving with yogurt or whipped fresh cream
and a sprinkling of finely chopped lovage.

Lovage Dumplings

(Good on any consommé or serve on beef stew)
½ cup flour
Pinch of salt
1 Tbs. butter
1 large egg
1 Tbs. chopped lovage

Sift flour and salt into a bowl. Cut in the butter in small pieces.
Beat the egg with the chopped lovage and stir into the flour
mixture. Beat until smooth. Drop small teaspoonfuls of the mixture
into a broad pan of boiled salted water. Cover and boil gently for
10 minutes. Lift out with a slotted spoon and serve. I also serve
this with the chicken stock above with the pieces of chicken added.
This makes a great winter meal.

Lovage Sauce for Fish

Melt 1 Tbs. butter or margarine in a saucepan over medium heat.
Stir in 2 Tbs. flour until smooth. Add 8 oz. milk and stir until
thickened. Into 10 oz. of this white sauce, fold a level Tbs. finely-
chopped lovage leaves. Also excellent over fresh garden beets.

Lovage & Cheese Soufflé

3 Tbs. butter
3 Tbs. flour
1 cup milk
Dash of hot pepper sauce
¼ tsp. dry mustard
4 Tbs. finely chopped lovage (smaller leaves)
1 cup grated cheddar cheese (or Colby or Jack)
5 eggs, separated
¼ tsp. cream of tartar

Melt butter in a saucepan. Add flour, stirring with a whisk. Heat
milk in another saucepan, then slowly add to the roux, stirring
constantly until well blended. Add hot pepper sauce, mustard and
lovage and blend in. Simmer for 2-3 minutes until the mixture
thickens. Add cheese and stir until the cheese melts and is well
blended. Remove saucepan from heat and add egg yolks. Stir until

blended and set aside. Beat egg whites in a bowl with the cream of tartar until they are stiff. Gently fold egg whites into cheese mixture. Put mixture in a buttered souffle´ dish and bake at 375° F. for 35 minutes or until risen and the top is lightly golden brown. Serve immediately.

Lovage & Carrot Salad
(Serves 4)

1 medium-to-large carrot, scrubbed and finely grated
1 large apple, peeled and grated
1 Tbs. finely chopped lovage
4 oz. yogurt
2 Tbs. mayonnaise
Salt to taste
Lettuce leaves
1 white onion, peeled, then sliced into rings

Toss the grated carrot and apple with the lovage and the yogurt, mayonnaise and salt. Arrange the lettuce leaves on a serving plate and mound some of the carrot, apple and lovage mixture onto each leaf. Separate the onion rings and arrange over the salad. Then decorate with a few whole lovage leaves and chill. Of course you can use low-fat yogurt and mayonnaise for a healthier salad.

Lovage with Vegetables
1 medium onion
¼ cup butter
6 carrots, small
6 parsnips, small
6 turnips, small
4 ½ cup chicken stock
Salt and pepper
¼ cup sour cream
3 Tbs. chopped lovage

Slice onion thinly and simmer gently in the butter. Add other vegetables thinly sliced. Cook about 8 minutes and add the heated stock. Season to taste and simmer covered for 20 minutes or until vegetables are slightly soft, not mushy. Pureé briefly in a blender, and return to pan. Reheat, adjust the salt and pepper, and add sour cream. Stir in chopped lovage and let stand for a few minutes.

Lovage Meat Balls

1 ½ lb. ground beef
½ lb. ground pork
1 egg
Fresh black pepper
¼ tsp. mace
¼ tsp. ginger
½ cup fresh bread crumbs
2 Tbs. butter
¼ cup flour
1 ½ cup hot water
1 ½ cup plain yogurt
3 Tbs. finely-chopped lovage leaves

Mix meats, egg and spices and bread crumbs together in a bowl. With wet hands, form mixture into meatballs about the size of a golf ball. Brown in a 450° F. oven on a jellyroll pan for 10 minutes. Remove from oven, drain and save any drippings, and place meatballs in a casserole dish. Place drippings in a skillet and add butter. Add flour, stirring constantly with a whisk. Slowly add water stirring until sauce is thick and smooth. Add yogurt and stir in lovage. Pour sauce over meatballs in casserole dish. Bake for 30 minutes at 350° F. Sprinkle with fine lovage and serve with broad noodles.

Opened-faced Lovage Sandwiches

Cut the crust off several slices of dark rye bread. Spread each slice with softened cream cheese and sprinkle with finely chopped lovage. Cut slices into triangles.

Lovage Skin-Cleansing Cream

Crush 1 ounce of lovage leaf in 1 cup of water and pour into a
ceramic pot. Add another cup of water and cover; slowly bring to a
boil and then simmer for a few minutes. Turn off the heat and let
the herbs infuse, covered, until cool. Strain this infusion and store
the water in the refrigerator.

1 oz. lanolin
½ oz. beeswax
3-4 oz. fruit oil (almond, avocado or soybean)
1 oz. of lovage water

In a double boiler, melt the lanolin and beeswax together. Add the
oil slowly, combining thoroughly. Remove the mixture from the
heat and whisk in the herb water, incorporating it thoroughly into
the cream. If you prefer something more like a lotion than a cream,
do not add the beeswax; use either lanolin or cocoa butter and
increase the herb water to 2 oz. If you wear makeup, cleanse your
skin with the lovage cleansing cream; it will remove makeup more
efficiently and more thoroughly than soap. The cream will leave a
light emollient film on the skin to keep moisture in, protecting skin.

Bath Vinegar

½ cup warm water
½ cup vinegar
2 Tbs. lovage, snipped in small pieces

Let the snipped lovage leaves steep in the water and vinegar mix
overnight or longer. Use fresh in your bath for a relaxing soak.

Bath Bag

Sew a 4-inch by 4-inch piece of cloth on three sides into a bag
leaving a tunnel for a long drawstring around the top (or use an old
washcloth and tie with a shoelace). Fill with fresh or dried lovage
seeds, leaves and/or stems. You may hang it on the bath faucet for
the water to run over or hang it on the showerhead. The bag may
also be used as a washcloth.

OTHER NOTES _____

Tuck lovage leaves into your boots or shoes when they are in storage to help keep them fresh.

In earlier times, combining lovage, yarrow leaves and sugar and then steeping in warmed brandy made a love potion. Because lovage leaves look like a larger form of flat-leafed parsley, this potion was called "love parsley."

The magnificent swallowtail butterfly especially likes the lovage plant on which to hatch its eggs into caterpillars. As I noted earlier, they are attracted to dill and fennel as well.

Culpepper treated ailments of the throat and neck with lovage compresses as well as using lovage tea after an excessive meal. He added lovage, called "an herb of the sun," to his list of herbal tonics, which were given for quinsy, a severe inflamation of the throat.

NOTES

SAGE

Wise And Healthful

SAGE

An ancient Chinese proverb asks, "How can a man grow old who has sage in his garden?" Another charm popular in Medieval times states, "Trefoil, johnswort, vervaine, dill, Hinder witches of their will, If the sage bush thrives and grows, The master's not master, and he knows."

Sage means esteem and it derives its scientific name from the Latin, *'salvere,'* to save, for its supposed powers to heal. The name was corrupted in Old English to 'sawge,' which has become the present day name of sage. The genus, which is very large, consists of herbs whose leaves are generally of a rugose appearance, and of a very aromatic smell. Traditionally associated with longevity, sage has a reputation for restoring failing memory and promoting long life and good health. This is one of the herbs most in demand in America.

 ## BOTANICAL NAME _____

There are over 900 species throughout the world in this large *salvia* genus with about 200 currently recognized as worthy to cultivate in gardens. They are widely grown throughout the world and cover all major uses (culinary, medicinal, cosmetic, decorative, aroma-therapy and dyes), except perhaps as a detergent. *Salvia* is of the *Lamiaceae* family.

Broadleaf or Garden Sage (common) – <u>*Salvia officinalis*</u> – is a culinary herb, a medicinal herb and a decorative plant. The silvery, gray-green, pointed leaves grow quickly and thickly, filling places in the herb garden in a way that slower growing herbs may not. Its mauve-blue spikes flower in May and June. This variety has the best flavor because of a good balance of volatile oils. The purple, tri-color and golden sages are prettier to look at, and I grow them all, but the extra camphor in their oils can substantially diminish the taste of a recipe.

Broad-leafed Sage – _S. o. broad-leafed_ – This hardy evergreen grows to two feet tall. Very rarely does it flower in cool climates, but the leaves are green with a texture larger than the ordinary sage. This species is propagated only from cuttings.

Purple Sage – _S. o. 'Purpurascens Group'_ – Even though this plant is commonly used in cooking, it does impose more of the camphor flavor. This tender evergreen grows to a compact 18 inches with infrequently blooming mauve-blue flowers in summer. The textured leaves are thin and oval-shaped and aromatic with the traditional sage scent. These narrow suede leaves are dull bottle-green suffused with inky purple. They are gently furred with short, silky hairs that give them a silvery bloom in certain lights, making them great mixers with many varieties and intensities of color. This species can be grown from cuttings or layering. Generally used in medicine, it has excellent healing properties in its aromatic purple foliage. It is also frequently used as a garnish and in herbal wreaths.

Red Sage – _S. miltriorrhiza_ – is said to be the most effective sage plants used medicinally. It is also known in China as dan shen (or Tan Shen) and is very important in Chinese medicine as a tonic herb. With its leaves of a maroon color, red sage should not be confused with red-flowering salvia seen frequently in park plantings.

Silver-Leafed Sage – _S. fruiticosa_ – may survive the hot, humid conditions in the South. This low shrub of silver-green foliage reaches to a height of three feet with a spread almost as large. Stems are square and woody with a woolly covering. The leaves, which have a rough appearance but downy texture, grow from the stems in an opposite arrangement. They can be up to three inches long. The species has a blue-lavender flower and does not propagate from seed.

Rosebud or Roseleaf Sage – _S. involucrata_ – is a zone 9 perennial which gives late fall color to the garden. This is an excellent hummingbird plant that grows to three or four feet and is covered with attractive deep rose tubular flowers but is not very aromatic. This plant is woody at the base, has medium green, smooth leaves and magenta flowers.

Golden Sage – _S. o 'Aurea'_ – has gold and green variegated leaves that make a striking plant in the garden. At 18 inches tall it is compact with dense growth and very showy.

Golden Variegated Sage – _S. o. 'Icterina'_ – is similar to aurea. It has light green leaves with gold margins. It is a perennial but some-what tender. Growing 12-18 inches high, it very rarely flowers in cool climates.

Tricolor Sage – _S. o 'Tricolor'_ – has colorful variegated leaves textured with cream, purplish, red and pink, all on the same leaf. This coloring is its outstanding feature. This favorite variety grows about 12-30 inches high. Its flower spires rise five inches or so above the pebbled foliage. Plants are a mass of intense blue-lavender flowers in the spring. Its foliage makes it essential for decorative purposes, but it can be used in cooking as well. The tricolor sage plant is somewhat tender in its hardiness but highly aromatic.

White-flowered Sage – _S. o. 'Albiflora'_ – is a "common sage" but unusual with its white flowers. It also has wonderful flavor in its gray-green leaves. This quite rare plant is hardy and grows to 24-30 inches.

Pink-flowered Sage – _S. o. 'rubriflor'_ – is another variety of common sage. It has good flavor in cream sauces because it's more delicate and also quite hardy.

Scarlet Sage – _S. coccinea_ – is an old-fashioned fire-engine-red sage. It reseeds readily but is sensitive to the cold and is usually grown as an annual. There are many named forms.

Blue Sage – _S. clevelandii_ – has beautiful sweet-scented blue flowers in spring and summer and is a shrubby perennial. Standing at three to four feet tall and almost as wide, it is larger than most other varieties. This native of southern California has silvery foliage that possesses a pleasant, warm flavor. Its woodsy aroma makes it a great candidate for dried bouquets or as a potpouri ingredient. It is hardy to 25° F.

Black Sage – *S. mellifera* – These aromatic leaves can be brewed into a tea. Early settlers in California used them to season sausage, poultry, and meat stuffing.

Pineapple Sage – *S. elegans* – has brilliant red flowers in the fall and makes a good winter houseplant. This variety prefers some shade. Leaves are green with a slight red tinge to the edges and have a glorious pineapple scent. Fresh or dried leaves can be used as a mild-flavored substitute for common sage. An infusion of the leaves is used as a substitute for tea but it does not hold its flavor well after high heat. It is good combined with apricots as stuffing for pork. This tender perennial grows two to three feet tall and will grow well indoors with good light. This plant grows only from cuttings, but I recently took 35 cuttings from my greenhouse plant and they all have taken and created new plants. Its distinctive pineapple-like fragrance and flavor make it a welcome addition to fruit salads, desserts, and cold drinks.

Fruit-scented Sage – *S. dorisiana* – is a tender plant but very vigorous and large, growing to five feet. It has a strong, sweet, mixed fruity aroma and very large velvety leaves and shocking pink flowers. This tender perennial is used in potpourris and other fragrant concoctions. It needs good light but also makes an attractive houseplant. It needs pinching to keep it bushy.

Clary Sage – *S. sclarea* – This most unusual and showy sage is a hardy biennial two to three feet tall. When planted in a bed with other varieties, the Clary sage towers above the lower growing sages nearby. Huge, pebbly gray-green leaves are often eight to nine inches long and slightly wrinkled. The young tender leaves of this sage may be dipped in cream, fried and eaten with sugar and orange sauce, or dipped in egg batter and fried as fritters (see Recipes). Finely-chopped leaves are cooked in soups and omelets. The leaves are added to Rhine wine to impart a muscatel taste and to flavor vermouth, beer, ale and liqueur as well. As a biennial, Clary sage does not flower the first year; instead, the plants form a rosette of light green corrugated, triangular, scallop-edged leaves on hairy purplish stalks. The next year, the plants produce numerous spikes of small flowers, each with a hook-shaped light blue upper part and a trough-like white lower part. Each tier of two-to-six flowers sits above a pair of large, papery whitish bracts edged with purple. They smell terrible up close. The ornamental flowers have a pleasant taste and can be sprinkled on a tossed salad.

Meadow Clary – _S. pratensis_ – This pungent, bitter flavored herb was formerly used for flavoring beer and wine. With lavender-blue flowers and low water needs, it makes a fine border plant.

Painted Sage – _S. viridis_ – is also a fine border plant. This annual is a soft gold-green with variegated leaves and purple or pink bracts. An infusion made from the leaves has been used for sore gums. The leaves and seeds increase the inebriating quality of liquors when added during fermentation.

Spanish Sage – _S. lavandulifolia_ – is a narrow-leafed sage. This hardy evergreen perennial stands eighteen inches tall. It has attractive blue flowers in summer and the leaves are green with a texture, small thin and oval in shape and highly aromatic. Because this sage is quite pungent, it is an excellent sage for cooking. It also makes a very flavorful tea. Its essential oil is used commercially to flavor ice cream, candy, baked goods, chewing gum, soft drinks, and alcoholic beverages.

Mealy Cup Sage – _S. farinacea 'Victoria'_ – Treated like an annual except in zones 9 and 10, this sage has silvery little bracts holding sapphire blue florets. These Mexico-Texas natives may live through a mild winter.

Autumn Sage – _S. greggii_ – is also very tender even though it's sometimes labeled for zone 8. They have many showy flowers and little leaves on a shrubby-like plant. This is a very attractive sage.

Mexican Bush Sage – _S. leucantha_ – is a four-foot plant with gray-green-silver foliage with spikes of lavender flowers. The long leaves smell like cocoa. Although it is not winter hardy, the flowers produce in abundance and dry well but also make a good cut flower that outlasts most others.

Russian Sage – _Perovskia atriplicifolia_ – is not really a sage, and not even Russian, but rather a native of Afghanistan and Pakistan. This plant is very versatile as an ornamental and was honored as the perennial plant-of-the year for 1995. Its beautiful purple-blue flowers dry well for floral arrangements. The leaves are pleasantly fragrant with a strong camphor scent. It's nice in potpourri and is an excellent bee plant.

Jerusalem Sage – _Phlomis fruiticosa_ – is also not salvia, but is a member of the _Lamiacea_ family. This tender evergreen perennial has some culinary uses, but I like it because it is beautiful in the garden. I have been asked many times about my Jerusalem Sage and people are very surprised that it is not even a sage.

 ## HISTORY

Native to the northern Mediterranean coast, sage is widely cultivated as far north as Canada because it is so hardy. The Romans brought it wherever they went to settle. In addition to being thought to impart wisdom, it has long had the reputation of retarding old age and of restoring energy and failing memory. Arabians associated sage with immortality or at least longevity, and it was credited with increasing mental capacity. In Medieval times, a sage tonic was drunk for a long life. The Saxons used sage not only to flavor port wine and meat dishes, as we do today, but they often cooked the pungent herb with fish. The Romans gathered sage and had a ceremony in which they cleaned their clothes, washed their feet, and cleaned the sacrificial food before the ceremony could begin. They used a special knife, not iron, to cut sage because it reacted with iron salts.

Sage found its way to England from the monastery gardens of France and Switzerland as early as the fourteenth century. It is said that when the British started importing tea from China, the Chinese so valued the herb they would trade from two to four cases of tea for one of dried English sage. A delicately colored cheese of seventeenth-century England was called sage cheese, and the modern Dutch, Swiss, and American sage cheeses are sold in our own food shops today. English stuffing and sauces were flavored with sage, especially those stuffings used with geese, veal, and whole roasted pigs. (See the Culinary Uses section for a further explanation).

Sages are grown all over the world from the mountains and deserts to everywhere in between, and from medium temperature ranges to hot and cold climates. Fields of sage in Yugoslavia are planted and harvested like wheat or hay, three crops a year, and used for cooking. America cannot cultivate enough sage for home consumption and annually imports thousands of tons of Dalmatian sage, which grows wild on the rocky hills of Yugoslavia.

American Indians used dried sage bundles for 'smudging' because of its clean aroma and silvery smoke. The smoking bundles were waved around rooms for purifying of homes or people. These trails of smoke would disperse and remove any gloomy or unfriendly feelings that were present, making people feel better, happier, and lighter.

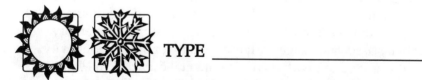 TYPE _____

The salvia genus can include annuals, biennials and perennials. Some salvias are herbs, some shrubs and some are sub-shrubs. They are generally very hardy and the most common sage plants will last for years. These plants are tough and need only moderate care. Clary sage, however, is a biennial, while pineapple sage is a tender perennial. Sage grown in the hot and humid south is sometimes used as an annual.

DESCRIPTION

Sage is an evergreen, woody shrub that is relatively tall, 24-30 inches, with pale purple flowers that bloom freely mid-summer in its second year. The nectar-filled flowers are very attractive to bees and butterflies. Flowers can be pink, purple, blue, red or white depending on the variety. The scent and flavor are as aromatic as that of lavender, without the sweetness and with their own curious dry pungency. Its fruit is an oval nutlet and its wiry stems are square and covered with down or felt. Although most sage blooms in mid-summer, it can sometimes bloom in autumn, or in spring depending on the weather. The oblong pewter-gray leaves are honeycombed with minute veins, giving them a grainy feel or pebbly effect. These are great garden plants because of the variety of silver-gray-blue-to-green foliage and many different colored flowers and bracts. Common sage is cold hardy to -10° F. and it has a pungent, bitter, cool and drying affect.

Ted Andrews, President and co-owner of HerbCo in Duvall, Washington states that golden and purple sages are really beautiful. However, the Bergartten sage is mostly left alone by slugs, has a milder flavor, can be harvested until almost Christmas time. HerbCo has been selling fresh herbs year-round to the Safeway, QFC and Fred Meyer stores in the Pacific Northwest since 1993.

Pineapple and Clary sage are taller than *officinalis*. Clary sage grows from two to three feet with handsome dusty green leaves. It is very showy in early summer covered with tiny lavender flowers.

PLANTING & CARE REQUIREMENTS___

In addition to being outstanding in the kitchen, sage varieties are beautiful ornamental plants in the garden. I grow several colorful species in one area for a dramatic background for some of my smaller herb plants. These excellent drought-tolerant plants are very suitable for home gardens. Give your sage all the heat and light you can, but they also need quick drainage and shelter from the wind.

Painted sage or Clary sage seeds can be started indoors six to eight weeks before the expected last frost. I sow seeds on the surface of a good seed mix in my greenhouse. A prepared seed plug tray, after planting, can be covered with perlite but doesn't need to be covered at all. The seeds need light to germinate, and it will take only about five days at temperatures from 65-75° F. Garden sage is sown in the same manner and will germinate in nine days. Sage seed may be sown in spring and autumn directly into the garden soil. The well-drained garden soil should be slightly alkaline (ph of 6.2 to 6.4) for sage plants but little moisture will be needed once the plants are established. Sage rarely needs fertilizing if the soil has good organic matter added. They do like a fair amount of nitrogen with adequate calcium; add some lime if calcium content is low. These plants will be happy in full sun but they can grow well in a semi-shady climate as well. The sunlight brings out the rich, volatile oils and valuable mineral substances. The flavor of sage does not deteriorate with the age of the plant, but plants vary in flavor, depending on soil and weather conditions. The flavor of fresh sage has unique lemon-rind tones over resin. The lemon flavor recedes and the camphor, along with a pleasant muskiness similar to silage, comes forward when sage is dried. A dried sage blend from Yugoslavia, marketed as "Dalmatian," is esteemed because the camphor odor is mild.

Sage grown in the garden does not suffer much from pests. Some mealy bugs, spider mites, spittlebugs and white flies can be a problem but the use of soapy water or Safer Soap can eliminate them. Grown in containers, especially pineapple sage, these plants can be prone to red spider mite. As soon as you see this pest, treat also with soap. A problem in our area during wet times is slugs. It is best to handpick these critters and dispose of them.

Fungus disease can be a problem if plants are grown too close together. Allow two to three feet between plants for fighting this problem. Black spot, a fungal disease, is more attracted to the plants if 'wet feet' are allowed to continue. Mulching sage plants with an inch or two of coarse sand will limit the spread of soil-borne wilt diseases where these are a problem. Wilt may strike at nearly any time, but is particularly noticeable during warm and wet springs. The disease attacks an entire branch or section of the plant, causing it to appear to wilt. Cut and dispose of affected branches. Do not replant sage where it has grown previously. Another fungus that attacks foliage causes it to brown first at the edges and then suddenly at an entire leaf or group of leaves. This is particularly troublesome in late summer and fall when a plant, usually a variegated variety, may be so weakened as to be destroyed by even a mild winter. Plants in damp heavy soil are subject to root rot and often die out in cold winters.

To discourage disease, keep plants pruned to encourage air circulation. Clean up any dead leaves around or under the plant. Keeping cabbage moths away from cabbage family plants is another bonus if you plant herbs and vegetables together. Sage also helps to repel cabbage butterfly and is said to improve the flavor and digestibility of cabbages if grown amongst them. When watering sage by hand (you can't help the rain), water near the base so water droplets don't spot the leaves when the sun comes out.

The silver-gray foliage of garden sage or the purple-mauve mix in purple sage is a nice ornamental especially when planted along with *Artemisia*, one of the mainstays of wreath makers. Sage and rosemary aid each when planted together.

Sage is an excellent herb for tub or container planting, as the soil and light requirements can be controlled, and its shape is well suited to large planters. An established sage needs little care aside from occasional pruning and watering. These plants may be kept to manageable proportions in an outside window box by harvesting the leaves and trimming back the woody stems as necessary. Trim it to twelve inches to keep it from being too shaggy. If the stems become spindly looking, the plant needs more light. Don't over-water the pots, but feed lightly after picking. Sage will grow indoors in pots but does need a window that has six hours of sun a day - or use artificial growing lights.

 ## HARVESTING

There are two methods of pruning and harvesting sage. After the first year, as many as two or three small harvests may be made during the growing season prior to flowering. Plants can be pruned in the early spring to encourage new growth, and it's best to harvest in the afternoon when the essential oil content is at its peak. Pinch off the top five inches of each stem. In summer, trim back after flowering. Pinch out the growing top when leggy or cut plants back. Mature plants can be pruned hard in the spring after some cuttings have been taken as insurance. Plants with woody stems like sage are best cut back to the previous year's growth level unless it is a new plant. If pruned frequently, it will maintain its bushy appearance. Since sage is an evergreen plant, leaves can be used fresh anytime of the year. The flowers may also be picked and used in a variety of ways. See the Culinary Uses for some good ideas.

Although many experts advocate this early spring pruning, you may inadvertently prune off the buds of forming flower spikes. I have found that light pruning in the early fall leaves the plant tidy and prepared for winter. Without so many leaves on the plant in winter there is less chance for pests to invade. You might wish to check the plant every few weeks in fall and winter and remove any dead branches. You can continue to harvest leaves through the winter, but the newer leaves in the spring and summer are much fresher tasting.

If you clip the purple sages in the spring, they develop new leaves and look really good but will flower only a small amount. If you do not clip them and allow it to flower it will become woody. If you cut it back in the fall, they will not produce new growth until the spring, so they can look a bit bare. If the plants are new and you wish to hold them over the winter, the last fall harvest (the only harvest in the first year) should be no later than September and should be a light one. In subsequent years, two or three harvests are possible

 ## PRESERVATION

 Although sage is an evergreen perennial and available year around, I do dry a supply in the fall. When we have had a particularly wet season, the leaves will dry greenish in color; in a very dry season the leaves will be gray. The leaves may even blacken when drying if the process is not done quickly under a steady airflow. Leaves dry well but you need to insure their green color as much as possible. Because this herb is frequently seen in its dried state, people presume it is easy to dry. But beware; although other herbs may lose some of their aroma or qualities if badly dried or handled, sage seems to pick up a musty scent and a flavor really unpleasant to taste. If you wish to dry the leaves for full flavor, use the pickings from the early pruning before the plant flowers. Pick these leaves in the morning after the dew has evaporated from them. Sage should be dried in a warm, dry place away from sun.

Cut herb branches, tie in bundles and hang in the shade, or lay the branches on airy racks. Or you may snip the leaves from branches you have removed, discard the stems, and spread the leaves on cloth or paper in the shade. I use a wooden dehydrator (Living Foods Dehydrator) with excellent results. I dry herbs at 90°-95° F. At this temperature the volatile oils are nicely preserved while drying time is very fast. Sage can be dried in the microwave (*see the Lovage chapter), but beware that sage can actually ignite. The dried herb has a stronger flavor, but a different taste, than the fresh sage does. It is not as lemony-tasting as fresh sage and might even taste musty. When the leaves are completely dry, store them whole in airtight containers. If you dry leaves on stalks, pack the dried stalks into boxes or jars and close tightly. Sage should be crumbled, never ground, at the last minute as needed for cooking; grinding completely destroys the delicate lemony perfume, leaving the harsher resinous flavors.

Common sage keeps its aroma and flavor through cooking and drying better than most culinary herbs. Dwarf sage, white-flowered sage, and purple sage are all handsome varieties of common sage with good flavor and aroma. Pineapple sage, fruit-scented sage, and mint-leaf sage all belong to the sage genus and have the familiar muskiness, with the added aromas that their names suggest. These varieties lose a bit of their perfume when dried, and most of it when cooked. They do have their place in the kitchen for flavoring beverages and jellies, and with fruits and desserts.

 ## PROPAGATION

Sage can be propagated by seeds, cuttings, divisions, and layering. As described under the Planting and Care Requirements, some sage is easy to grow from seed, and annual sage must be grown from seed. However, golden, red, purple and tricolor sage needs to be propagated by cuttings. Sage seeds store poorly and you should test its germination before planting a large amount. Fortunately, seeds germinate quickly, so you will soon know whether or not they are responding. Sow these viable seeds in late spring and transplant to two feet apart when the seedlings reach three inches. If the seeds are viable, you will get a 60-70% germination rate. For the first winter, cover the young plants with mulch if you are in a colder climate. You may want to start plants from cuttings or by division because it takes two years to grow good-sized plants from seed.

Taking cuttings is a good method for the variegated species and those that do not set seed in cool climates. Take softwood cuttings in late spring or early summer from the strong new growth. All varieties take easily from cuttings with rooting occurring in about four weeks in summer. Cuttings are more successful if the 'felty' layer on the lower stem is rubbed off. By using the more tender stems, sage can also be propagated from four-inch cuttings taken in the fall for use the following spring. See the Propagation section in the Lemon Verbena chapter for more details.

I have been successful with layering sage branches when the plants become large and woody. In September, I simply pin a branch to the soil with an opened large paper clip. I give it some water and in a few weeks, depending on the weather, the branch has formed roots. I cut the original plant from the new stem and remove the old plant completely. When these new roots have adequately grown in the spring, I dig up the plant and place it in its permanent home.

 MEDICINAL USES _____

The medicinal use of sage goes back hundreds, maybe thousands, of years. The purple variety of sage is generally used in medicine and is more effective than the common green plant. Because the plant is carminative, antispasmodic and astringent as well as antiseptic, it is and has been used in a myriad of potions, lotions, infusions, tonics and teas. It also contains a fair amount of antioxidants.

Its major volatile oils include thujone, camphor and eucalyptol. The leaves also contain bitter compounds, tannins (such as rosmarinic acid), flavonoids and substances with an antiperspirant and estrogen-like effect.

Red sage is useful for palpitations, can stabilize the heart, calms and strengthens the nerves and lightens stagnant blood. Used as a circulatory stimulant, it also clears excessive heat from the body. Roots are effective against angina pectoris, cerebral arteriosclerosis and phlebitis. Sage can reduce blood pressure, improve circulation by dilating the blood vessels and reduce blood cholesterol.

Drinking sage tea acts as a sedative and also can alleviate irritability and insomnia. It is especially recommended for older persons to banish melancholy and depression and restore ailing memory. The Chinese prefer sage tea to their own Chinese tea for aiding the digestion and other debilities of the stomach. They use it as a tonic made from a strong infusion. Clary sage, in particular, has been used for upset stomach and digestive system disorders for centuries. Mariners used sage for bouts of seasickness. It also has a healing effect for kidneys, may be used as a compress for swelling, ulcers, and boils, and is a good tonic for colds, coughs, headache and constipation.

Sage's camphor and other volatile oils have antiseptic properties which, when combined with the astringent action of sage's tannin, is the reason sage is good for treating sore throats, mouth irritations, gum disease and tonsillitis. It also cleans plaque and dental stains from the teeth. Removing plaque and tarter can be done by simply rubbing a sage leaf over the surfaces of the teeth and gums twice a day. Another method of cleansing the teeth is to add crumbled dry sage leaves to the paste on your brush. Swiss peasants used sage as a dentifrice, first chewing a few leaves, then brushing the gums with a twig. This will also whiten the teeth and aid in preventing gingivitis. Gargling with sage and vinegar will alleviate ulcerated gums, or sage and cloves can be used together to relieve toothache. Many commercial gargles and mouthwashes include the sage volatile oil as the main ingredient.

Sage in the bath is very soothing for aching muscles, abrasions, cut and bruises, infections and skin disorders like psoriasis, dermatitis and shingles. Sage lowers blood sugar in diabetics, treats constipation and liver ailments, and is a good general tonic. A strong sage tea (infusion) is very effective for stress and even shock as it relaxes peripheral blood vessels. It can also reduce perspiration, salivation and lactation, is a uterine stimulant, and can reduce night sweats in menopause. It is also good for general menstrual complaints.

Extended or excessive use of sage can cause symptoms of poisoning. Although the herb seems safe and common, if you drink the tea for more than a week or two at a time, its strong antiseptic properties can cause potentially toxic effects. Sage contains thujone, which can trigger fits in epileptics, who should avoid the herb. Several cups of sage tea a day taken as a therapeutic dose during pregnancy should also be avoided.

 OTHER USES

Sage is effective as a hair rinse to restore color to graying hair (see the Recipe section). Adding rosemary or stinging nettle to the infusion increases the darkening effect and prevents dandruff. Cleansing creams and lotions are popular products made with sage. In a facial steam (see Fennel) it creates a smooth, soft skin and in a facial pack it deep-cleans the pores. Clary sage soap cleanses deeply.

The same antiseptic qualities and tannic qualities that help heal sore mouth make sage tea a soothing after-shave splash. Make a batch of the tea and keep it covered in the refrigerator for up to a week. Splash it on cold, straight from the fridge just after shaving. To soften your skin, mix the brewed sage tea with an equal amount of aloe juice. Make an infusion by pouring a cup of boiling water over a handful of sage. Let it stand for ten minutes, strain and apply to the face to help close pores.

The volatile oils and tannins in sage are thought to account for its reputation for drying up perspiration. Garden sage is nice in sleep pillows because it acts as a sedative; pineapple sage for potpourri is wonderful because of its aroma.

Leafy sprigs of sage were among the strewing herbs spread with rushes on the floors of old manors. This was done because sage was believed to be an antiseptic against plague and other infections as well as keeping bugs and critters at bay. Sage branches make a great base for floral or herbal wreaths. I use it on both mossback and straw-back wreaths. Sage was an important ingredient in sausage stuffing as the volatile oils have a preservative effect on meat, a necessity before refrigeration.

Sage tops yield a yellow-buff color to wool. Sage has been smoked as tobacco. Clary sage oil distilled from the flower stems and leaves is used in toilet waters, perfumes, and to flavor wine, vermouth and liqueurs.

Throw herb branches, trimmings or spent leaves on the hot coals of your barbecue to add a smoky, herbal flavor to your favorite grilled item.

 **CULINARY USES** _____

Sage is a strong, culinary herb with lovely flavor to be used with discretion. Cooks and homemakers all over the world use this marvelously aromatic herb in many foods, such as appetizers, cheeses, fish, game, meats, poultry, bland cream soups, chowders, sauces, stuffing, and stews.

Sage is perhaps best known and loved of all American seasonings to cut the fatty taste in meals like pork and sausage, and for duck, goose, and rabbit. There is no comparison between the flavor of the freshly chopped tender leaves and the dried ones that lose much of their volatile oil if not dried correctly. Both the dried and the fresh whole leaves are universally used, and the powdered, dried sage is available in the markets. However, as I mentioned in the Preservation section, powdered sage loses its delicate lemony perfume. Sage is really an absolute necessity in the preparation of many prepared meats and sausages with its aromatically bitter and strong flavor. This is the magic ingredient that enhances turkey stuffing and permeates kitchens during the holiday seasons. The reason for such culinary use of sage in wild game, pork and poultry is not often considered, except that one assumes it is pleasant and spicy. Actually, sage is used in stuffing because it is effective as a carminative and as an aid in the digestion of rich dishes. It helps to carry away the fat from the poultry instead being retained as cellulite!

One of my favorite uses for fresh sage leaves is to add it in a grilled cheese sandwich. The lemony, camphor-like, and pine flavor mixes pleasantly with the sharpness of cheddar cheese. As well as using in a grilled cheese sandwich, try minced leaves in cream cheese for spreads on toast or crackers or in cottage cheese. Use fresh sage leaves to make oils, vinegars and French salad dressing. Eat fresh leaves in salads and mince in omelets, fritters, yeast breads, marinades, and meat pies. A particular virtue of sage is its ability, whether fresh or dried, to enliven heavier food. The aromatic spiciness combines well with robust dishes, and its nutritional contribution is high. Because it holds up so well in cooking, try it with liver, beef, fish, lamb, veal, duck or goose paté, artichokes, stewed tomatoes, asparagus, brussel sprouts, and cabbage. I have also liked the results with oranges, lemons, garlic, lentils and shell beans, and it combines well with dairy foods. Make slits in pork roast and place fresh shredded sage leaves in the slits with garlic before roasting. Mince leaves and use in breading for fried chicken. Try minced sage on squash or sweet potatoes and forego the butter or add some minced fresh sage to tomato or vegetable soup. Try pairing sage with onion, garlic, shallot, or leeks since its strong flavor holds up well to these strong ingredients. Sage is a wonderful addition to pizza - not just oregano and basil!

Carrots, peas, string beans, eggplant and butter sauce all taste better with sage leaves. Flavored sage like Clary and pineapple can stand in for regular sage with almost any food. Pineapple sage is excellent torn into pieces in a salad or fruit cup. Try stuffing pineapple sage leaves under the skin of a whole chicken before roasting. These lighter sages do not hold up as well in high-heat cooking.

The sage flowers, whether lavender, blue or red, have an excellent flavor and should be used as well. The flowers of the following sage plants are edible: broad-leafed, purple, golden, golden variegated, tricolor, pineapple, and fruit-scented. I mince them and use in herbal butter or on a melon salad. Of course, they always make great presentations when simply sprinkled over pasta or on the side of a plate.

Sufferers from flatulence and indigestion may be helped if they eat a sandwich with fresh or dried sage, or drink a cup of sage tea, which is a pleasing and beneficial drink. With thyme and marjoram, it is a traditional mix for many culinary dishes. For fresh sage chips, sauté leaves in butter over medium heat until crisp, drain and salt. Use on the side of the plate as a garnish or as an appetizer.

 ## RECIPES

From the number of recipes in this section, you can see it is one of my favorite herbs, not only for cooking, but medicinal and cosmetic uses as well.

Sage Fritters (a light appetizer)
50 sage leaves, about 2 inches long
¾ cup all-purpose flour
½ tsp. salt
4 Tbs. olive oil
2 Tbs. dry white wine
½ cup water
2 large egg whites
Vegetable oil for frying

Brush the sage leaves clean. Wash them only if necessary and be sure they are completely dry before battering them. Mix the flour and salt together in a bowl. Whisk the water, then the olive oil and wine into flour to make a smooth batter. Cover the batter with plastic wrap and let it stand for an hour or two at room temperature or in the refrigerator overnight. Let the batter come to room temperature before using it. When you are ready to cook the fritters, heat one inch of peanut or other vegetable oil to about 360° F. Beat the egg whites until stiff but not dry. Fold the beaten egg whites into the batter and place the batter in a shallow baking dish. Place about 1/3 of the sage leaves on the batter. Using kitchen tongs or a fork, coat the leaves with the batter. Drop the leaves by the stems individually into the hot oil. Cook the fritters until they are golden brown, turning them once after about 1-½ minutes. Remove from the oil and drain on paper towels. Keep warm in a 150° F. oven. Continue coating and frying the leaves until all have been cooked. Serve the fritters hot with lemon wedges on the side.

Eggs with Sage
1 tsp. olive oil
1 tsp. butter
6 large fresh sage leaves
3 large eggs, whisked
2 Tbs. freshly grated Parmesan cheese

Heat the oil and butter in a medium nonstick sauté pan over medium high heat until the butter has just melted. Swirl the pan to mix the oil and butter evenly. Arrange the sage leaves in the pan and let them sizzle for about 20 seconds or until fragrant. Pour the eggs over the sage leaves and immediately sprinkle on the cheese. Rotate the pan so the eggs cook evenly. When the mixture sets (in about 2 minutes) slide the omelet onto a warm plate flipping over in half to continue to cook the inside. Garnish with sage flowers or other herbs. Serves 2.

Garlic Soup with Sage, Fennel and Parsley
2 quarts water
1 whole head of garlic, cloves separated, but unpeeled
1 tsp. salt
Pinch of pepper
Large handful of herbs (sage, parsley, fennel, rosemary, thyme, chives and anything else you find fresh)
2 egg yolks
3 Tbs. olive oil

Place the first five ingredients in a saucepan, bring to a boil, and then simmer gently for 30 minutes. Strain out the solids and return the soup to the pan. Beat 2 egg yolks with a whisk, and then beat into them 3 Tbs. of olive oil. Whisk a small amount of the hot soup into the egg yolk mixture, then another ladle full. Add the yolk blend back into the soup pot, stirring as you go. You may add leftover creamed or mashed potatoes to this soup. (This garlic soup is great for colds or influenza.)

Butternut Squash Soup
(This low-fat nutritious soup uses no milk or cream for its base)

1 medium butternut squash, peeled, halved, seeded and chopped into ½ inch pieces
4-5 cups poultry broth (defatted)
3 medium potatoes, peeled and chunked
2 large carrots, sliced
6 cloves garlic, peeled
1 Tbs. fresh sage or 1 tsp. dried
1 Tbs. fresh basil or 1 tsp. dried
½ Tbs. fresh thyme or ½ tsp. dried
½ cup dry red wine
1 tsp. Tamari sauce
Freshly ground black or white pepper

In a soup pot over medium-high heat, combine the squash, broth, potatoes, carrots, and garlic. The water should just cover the vegetables. Bring to a boil, lower heat to medium and cook 15 minutes or until the vegetables are tender. Add the herbs, wine and Tamari and cook 5 minutes more. Purée the soup in a food processor or blender. Return to the pot and add pepper to taste. Reheat gently and serve.

Sage Cornbread
(This recipe is great with chili.)

1 cup flour
1 cup cornmeal
1 Tbs. baking powder
½ cup butter, melted
1 cup milk
1 egg
½ cup canned or frozen corn (drained)
1 ½ Tbs. chopped fresh sage

Preheat oven to 375° F. Mix flour, cornmeal and baking powder together. In another bowl mix butter (or margarine) milk, and egg together. Mix the liquid mixture into the dry. Stir until just blended. Stir in corn and sage. Place in a greased 8-inch square pan and bake for 20 minutes or until browned on top.

Sweet Potato Salad with Sesame-Sage Dressing

1 lb. sweet potatoes, peeled and cut into 2-inch chunks
3 lemon slices
½ tsp. maple syrup
2 Tbs. fresh lemon juice
1 shallot, finely minced
1 Tbs. dark sesame oil
2 Tbs. toasted sesame seeds
1 Tbs. minced fresh sage

Set the sweet potatoes over boiling water to which you've added the lemon slices, and steam until tender, about 12 minutes. Meanwhile, combine the maple syrup, lemon juice, shallot, sesame oil, sesame seeds, and sage in a medium bowl and stir well. Toss the sweet potato chunks with the dressing and serve warm or very slightly chilled.

Sage Pasta
(We like this served with Kielbasa or Polish sausage.)

2 cups flour
3 large eggs
½ tsp. fresh pepper
25 large, stemmed sage leaves
Coarse salt

Mound the flour on a pastry board and make a well in the center. Mix the eggs, salt, pepper and finely torn sage leaves and then place in the well. Begin incorporating the flour. When all the ingredients are blended, knead by hand until it becomes elastic. Put through a pasta machine as instructed. I like wide noodles. Or if you have a fully automatic pasta machine, mix and extrude in the machine. Serve with a simple sauce of butter, cheese and a little pasta water. Sprinkle sage leaves over the top.

Creamed Onions with Sage

¾ lb. of pearl onions (fresh or frozen)
2 Tbs. butter
1 Tbs. flour
¾ cup chicken stock (see Lovage chapter)
Salt and pepper
6 sage leaves
3 Tbs. heavy cream
Parsley, fresh chopped

Peel the onions if they are fresh but leave them whole. Heat the butter in a saucepan over medium heat and brown the onions gently, allowing 5 minutes (if thawed). Blend in the flour and cook one minute more then add the heated stock and stir until smooth. Add salt and pepper to taste and the chopped sage leaves. Cover the pan and simmer for 20 minutes stirring occasionally. When the onions are soft, stir in the cream and chopped parsley and serve.

Sage with Lamb

Prepare a leg of lamb several hours before cooking. Make several incisions across the top, then press a little finely-chopped garlic and crumbled dried sage, or chopped fresh sage, into each slit. Place the leg in a baking dish, pour 4 ounces of red wine over it; sprinkle with herb salt, cover with plastic and marinate for at least 5 hours. Place in a hot oven set at 400° F. to roast. After 30 minutes, spoon the wine in the dish over the meat, and add 4 ounces vegetable oil. Continue baking at 325° F. until the leg is cooked, (about 15 minutes per pound) basting occasionally. Vegetables may be placed around the joint the last 35 minutes of cooking time. The gravy made from the pan juice is dark brown and very tasty.

Pork Tenderloin Roast with Pineapple Sage

(My husband, Charles' favorite dinner!)

Marinade:
4 ounce pineapple juice
2 oz. Teriyaki sauce
2-3 cloves garlic, crushed
1 Tbs. grated ginger
2 Tbs. minced pineapple sage

Mix and marinate a two-to-three pound boneless pork tenderloin roast for 4-6 hours before roasting. Roast at 325° F. until internal temperature is 160° F.

Sage Tea

Pour 8 ounces of boiling water over 2 tsp. dried crumbled sage leaves or 1 Tbs. fresh leaves, torn. Cover and infuse, or steep, for several minutes. Strain and sweeten with honey if desired. Chop or tear the leaves before adding to the cup. This is a flavorful medicinal tea (see Medicinal Uses) or a pleasant beverage any time.

Sage Oil

Blanch about 2 cups fresh sage leaves in boiling water for just a few seconds, then refresh under ice cold water and pat dry. Place in a blender and add 2 tsp. of fresh lemon juice and 2 tsp. of sugar. Blend and add 2 cups of very good olive oil and a pinch of salt. Process till smooth. Place in a sterilized jar and refrigerate four days, then strain through a fine mesh strainer or cheesecloth and return oil to the jar. Flavored oils keep for about two weeks, refrigerated to prevent bacteria growth or botulism. Herb oils are wonderful as a dip for crusty bread, drizzled on salads, or added to vegetables or soups.

Sage Vinegar

1 cup sage leaves
½ cup parsley leaves
1 shallot, minced
1 qt. warmed red wine vinegar

Place herbs and shallot in a sterilized jar and add the warmed vinegar. Cap with a non-corrosive cap (such as a cork) and leave in the sun for a few days. You can decant or leave the herbs and shallots in the bottle.

Sage Jelly
(Try this with your morning sausages.)

4 Tbs. finely chopped sage
1 ¼ cups boiling water
¼ cup white wine vinegar (do not use distilled vinegar)
3 cups sugar
2 drops of green food coloring (optional)
½ bottle of liquid pectin

Put sage and boiling water in a saucepan and allow to steep for 15 minutes, covered. Use 1 cup of this strained liquid and place it in another saucepan. Add vinegar and sugar and bring to a boil. Add food coloring and pectin, stirring constantly. Remove saucepan from heat. Skim mixture and pour into hot, sterile jars. Seal and store.

Sage Honey Applesauce
6 large Macintosh apples, about 2 lb.
⅓ cup sage honey or ⅓ cup honey, unflavored, and 3 sage leaves
1-2 Tbs. fresh lemon juice

Core, peel and chop apples coarsely. Put them in a heavy saucepan and stir in the honey, sage leaves if you are using them, and lemon juice. Cover and cook over low heat for 30-40 min. until the apples have softened completely. Remove the sage leaves if they were used. Purée mix in a food mill or food processor. Let the sauce cool to room temperature. Serve at room temperature or cold.

Sage Apple Cake
2 cups white, all-purpose flour
1 tsp. baking soda
1 tsp. baking powder
½ tsp. salt
½ tsp. cinnamon
1 cup packed, plus 3 Tbs. light brown sugar
14 Tbs. unsalted butter (1 ⅔ cubes), softened
2 large eggs
1 Tbs. minced fresh sage

1 cup sage honey applesauce
1 large Macintosh, Winesap or other good cooking apple
1 Tbs. lemon juice

Sift the flour with the baking soda, baking powder, salt and cinnamon. Cream 1 cup brown sugar with 12 Tbs. butter. Beat the eggs into the creamed sugar and butter. Combine the sage with the applesauce and add to the butter mixture, beating well. Gradually add the flour mixture to the applesauce mixture, blending well. Preheat the oven to 350° F. Core the apple and slice it thin. Toss the slices with the lemon juice. Butter the bottom and sides, heavily, of a 9-inch bundt pan with the remaining 2-Tbs. butter. Sprinkle the bottom and sides of the pan with the remaining 3-Tbs. brown sugar. Arrange the apple slices around the bottom and sides of the pan. Pour the batter carefully into the prepared pan. Bake for 50-60 minutes on a rack until the top is a deep golden brown and a knife comes out clean. Cool the cake to room temperature before removing it from the baking pan. Loosen the sides of the pan and invert the cake on a serving platter.

Sage Gargle
(For sore throats, laryngitis and tonsillitis. Beneficial for infected gums and mouth ulcers.)

Pour a pint of boiling water over a handful of torn sage leaves and cover. When fairly cool, add a little vinegar and honey. Take a teaspoonful at a time for a sore throat or use ½ cup as a gargle.

Sage and Milk Gargle and Mouthwash
(Excellent for whitening the teeth and strengthening the gums)

Pour 8 ounces milk into a saucepan and add 2 tsp. crumbled dried sage (or 1 tablespoon chopped fresh sage). Bring slowly to a simmer, covered, and cool. Strain and use as a gargle or mouthwash. Or simply steep one teaspoonful of fresh sage in one cup of hot water, covered, for 4 minutes. Then swirl in a quarter teaspoon of salt and a teaspoon of cider vinegar. Swish the mixture around in your mouth while it's still hot and then spit it out.

Rinse for Dark Hair

Add 4 Tbs. sage and 2 Tbs. rosemary to 2 cups water. Simmer for
30 minutes. Strain and cool. Rinse through hair several times,
catching excess in a bowl. Rinse with clear water.

Gray Hair Rinse

Use recipe above but heat the rinse and leave on the hair for 20-30
minutes with your head wrapped in a towel. Use an old towel
because it will leave a dye stain behind. Do not rinse out. Do this
weekly to turn gray hair back to its natural dark color.

Sage Skin-Freshening Lotion

Purée fresh sage leaves with very cold water in an electric blender.
Dab on your face and neck using a cotton ball. Dried sage may also
be used. Add 1 cup of dried crushed sage to 1 pint of pure water in
a quart glass jar with a tight-fitting lid. Put this glass jar in a
convenient place and shake once or twice daily for two weeks.
Strain and store in small glass vials with lids. Sage is both
stimulating and an astringent to your skin.

 OTHER NOTES _____

Clary sage makes a good cutting flower. The fragrance can even
induce sleep using aromatherapy techniques or sleep pillows. The
plant is a beautiful backdrop in the garden for bright colored lilies
or roses.

As the subtle purple blooms of garden sage come in early to mid-
summer, the bees and butterflies are heavily attracted. Many sage
varieties, especially the bright red flowers of the pineapple sage,
make a good butterfly garden. Try golden sage to attract monarch
butterflies. Place flat rocks near the plants so that the butterflies
may warm themselves in the sun. They need this environment to
restore heat for flying, as they are cold-blooded. A sage garden
with a southern exposure with full sun in early afternoon is ideal.
Puddles of water nearby are helpful because the butterflies can use
the nutrients found in the water for nourishment.

When attracting bees, the result is a splendidly aromatic honey if you have a beekeeper nearby. Good insects and hummingbirds are attracted as well. Used also as insect repellent, sage in the garden sends away flies, cabbage moths and carrot flies.

Sage is a great Mediterranean herb to grow on a sunny windowsill in the kitchen. Soak an unglazed terra cotta or wooden pot in water first so that moisture isn't pulled from the soil. Dampen the potting soil and place sage and other herbs (basil, chives, oregano, marjoram, and parsley) alongside. Snip the plants regularly to keep them pruned and pretty. These plants won't grow as large as when they are in the garden, but you will have an immediate supply right at hand. If you transplant sage from the garden, the root system is likely to be larger than it would be if you purchased a small potherb. Therefore, you need to prune the root down to a small size after removing much of the soil. Tamp it down in the container and place soil within an inch of the top. A deeper container (8-12 inches) will garner a better root system than a more shallow pot.

And last but not least, sage also contains abundant sources of vitamins A, B1, B2, C, niacin, potassium, calcium and iron. And all of this from a plant with just one or two calories - that anyone can grow - almost anywhere! Wow, why wouldn't you want this wise and healthful plant?

NOTES: _____

SALAD BURNET
My Cucumber Substitute

SALAD BURNET

Salad burnet brings joy and a merry heart like borage, and has the power to drive away melancholy. Sometimes this herb is called garden burnet. The word burnet, meaning brunette or brown in Old French, refers to the brownish red flowers. This herb has not been in great demand in America. The plant is called di-yu in China.

 BOTANICAL NAME _____

Minor Burnet – _Sanguisorba minor_ or _Poterium sanguisorba_ – is not a well-known herb. _Poterium_ is from the Greek, _poterion_, meaning, 'drinking cup' referring to its use in cool drinks. The rest of the name, its old generic name, comes from _sanguis_ (blood) and _sorbere_, to staunch (or absorb). Salad burnet had a reputation for being able to stop bleeding; both leaves and the root were recommended. It belongs to the _Rosaceae_ family. There is another burnet too, not to be confused with this one, called _Pimpinella saxifraga_, which is of the same family as parsley and dill but is not used in cooking.

Greater Burnet – _Sanguisorba officinalis_ – is closely related to _s. minor_, but is a much taller perennial growing to four feet with a two-foot spread. It produces small spikes of dark crimson flowers in summer and has mid-green leaves that are divided into oval leaflets. Its medicinal and culinary uses are very similar.

 HISTORY _____

Salad burnet is native to Europe and Asia as far north as Norway and is now naturalized in North America and Britain as well as other places in the world. During the sixteenth century, the Golden Age of plant medicine, burnet was of great interest to herbalists. People believed that they were protected from the Plague when they drank white wine with dissolved burnet and twenty other herbs. This ancient herb has been grown in Great Britain since that time. In Tudor times, salad burnet was planted along the border of garden paths so the scent would rise when stepped on; it was also planted in knot gardens.

Four hundred years ago, burnet in salads was as common as cucumber is today. One of the most venerable of the forgotten herbs, it has been under-used medicinally for at least 2,000 years. Its medicinal powers were discovered in the first century A.D. Popular for both its medicinal and culinary properties, it was taken to New England by the Pilgrims. The Shakers mentioned using burnet in the 1820's for healing wounds. Burnet's leaves and roots have been used throughout American history. The wild roots were harvested and dried, then ground and boiled with water to make a tea.

Soldiers in the Revolutionary War drank boiled burnet root tea before battle to prevent extreme bleeding if they were shot. Thomas Jefferson planted fields of burnet for feed for his animals. And, of course, the human animals used it too, putting sprigs in glasses of wine for a merry celebration. It was also used in the spring as a tonic.

 TYPE _____

This is a very attractive perennial plant that is easy to grow and needs little care. It grows as a perennial in zones 3-10, but has difficulty in the humid, hot south where it is more like an annual. It's sad that herb gardeners do not better know burnet, but I hope to change that!

DESCRIPTION _____

Burnet is found in dry, free-draining soil in grasslands and on the edges of woodlands. This perennial herb looks like a loose clump of divided leaves and grows to two feet tall with a spread of about two feet. It's a very attractive herb for borders or edging a garden. When it is small it has blue-green rosettes of foliage. When older, it has oval-toothed leaflets and deep crimson flower heads, something like a clover head. The small round leaves look as if they have been cut out with pinking scissors and then fastened in eight or nine neat pairs along each side. The leaves are on a central stem. These soft, mid-green leaves are divided or compounded. Its form is like a spray that falls gracefully from the center outwards in an umbrella shape. Small new plants of this herb make a great centerpiece in a hanging herb basket.

The leaves have a fresh cucumber flavor; especially the young leaves that are the most tender. Leaves stay green during a mild winter. Although the leaves have no aroma when dried, the newly-picked foliage has a dewy, fresh flavor with a number of special uses.

In summer, many straight stalks quickly shoot upward bearing unusual raspberry-like flower heads about three-quarters inch across. Flowers have pink tufts of stigmas and dangling stamens, but no conspicuous petals. These rounded, crimson flower heads bloom for three months, from May through July. The lower flowers have only male flowering parts; middle flowers have both male and female parts; and the upper rings of flowers have just female parts. This is very unusual in the herb family.

PLANTING & CARE REQUIREMENTS__

Burnet is so hardy it will grow in all types of soil and under almost any conditions. Dry sandy loam in full sun or partial shade is ideal, but it will tolerate any well-drained soil in sun or light shade. It prefers a soil pH 6.8 and grows well even down to zone 3. It can't take extreme summer heat, but can last through even a cold winter for off-season greenery. Buy an organically grown plant and put it where it gets at least six hours of sun a day.

Seeds taken from last year's plant may be started indoors ten weeks before the last expected frost. Plant one-half inch deep as they need darkness to germinate. They should germinate in eight to ten days at 70° F. Seeds may also be started in the fall before the first frost. The seedlings may be transplanted out in the garden when they reach five to six inches high. Plant them where they will remain because they have a woody taproot and will not transplant well after reaching their full growth. They will self-sow when the flower seeds fall to the ground in late summer.

This very attractive soft-leaf herb is useful in both kitchen and garden. This evergreen is most effective as a garden edging plant. It also looks good in a wildflower garden, where it grows as happily as in its original grassland habitat. During dry summer weather, the plant will need watering, but don't overdo it. This herb is mainly free from pests and diseases. Mildew can be a problem if the leaves are kept too wet, so provide good air circulation in the planting bed. If the winter-time drainage is not very good, they can die of crown rot.

Indoors, burnet grows well in a wide clay pot. Clay keeps the soil drier than plastic and the roots need space to spread. It also needs six hours of sun a day indoors. Water regularly but not too frequently. Feed with liquid fertilizer in the spring only. Do not overfeed, or the leaf will soften and lose its cool cucumber flavor, becoming more like a spinach. Burnet grown indoors in a container is not as large or vigorous as one in the outdoor garden.

HARVESTING

When the flower stalks appear, they may be removed to the crown. This will keep the plant from flowering and help it to continuously supply fresh young leaves. Continue to cut the plant as it strives to go to flower. Once a new plant has started from seed, it is better to let that self-seeded plant become the dominant plant each year.

When harvesting the leaves, pick the leafy stems from the outside of the plant. The center of the plant is the area where new growth forms and should *not* be pinched out. After removing the stems - which are very fragile - hold the top end between your thumb and finger and simply slide it down to remove the leaves. This is much quicker than removing each leaf individually.

Erick and Paula Haakenson, owners of Jubilee Farm in Carnation, Washington, grow thirty varieties of herbs, including salad burnet. Their seven-year-old organic farm used to be a dairy farm, but they now supply many vegetables and herbs to the area. They harvest salad burnet fresh for their customers.

PRESERVATION

Fresh salad burnet does not preserve well by freezing or drying. The most popular way to preserve this herb is in vinegar. I use the chopped leaves along with chives to create herbal butter. (The vinegar and butter recipes are in the Recipe section.) This cucumber/onion flavor goes well with rye bread. I attempted to dry the herb once and it became dark and lost most of its flavor. When I have tried freezing the leaves, they were a little better, but still not on a par with the fresh leaves. Since we have little or no snow cover in winter, I can harvest them fresh all winter. If you have snow over a long period of time, you might wish to freeze a supply. The leaves seem to be even sweeter in the coldest winter months.

PROPAGATION _____

Sow the small, flatish seed directly into the garden in spring or autumn. You will get a germination rate of about 75%. Transplant about eighteen inches apart. If seeded in the autumn, protect the new seedlings during the first winter.

Salad burnet divides very easily. Dig up an established plant in the early spring or late autumn. Cut back any excessive leaves, divide the plant, and replant in a prepared site in the garden. You will need to divide your plants every three to four years to keep the leaves young and tasty. With the plant being hermaphroditic (both male and female), it is not necessary to have more than one plant for a continuous source. The flowers are wind pollinated.

 MEDICINAL USES _____

As is true with so many herbs, the specificity of modern science has failed to quantify the medical effectiveness of burnet, but it has been used for many centuries for several ailments. Salad burnet has long been associated with blood; *sanguisorba* means, literally, "drink up blood," and herbalists prepared a tea to stop hemorrhaging. A burnet tonic aids women going through a difficult menopause and helps with excess menstrual bleeding and cramps. For a remedy for menstrual cramps, prepare a strong infusion/tea, covered; steep five to ten minutes before drinking. I make this infusion/tea in my medicinal classes and there is almost always a woman present who is experiencing cramps. As a volunteer, the woman drinks the tea and always responds that the cramps are gone in just a few minutes.

The root is used to make an herbal ointment that is smoothed on wounds. Salad burnet has been a traditional remedy for hemorrhoids, diarrhea, dysentery, fevers and infections and as a mild diuretic stimulating kidney activity. Added to beer or wine, it is used to create relief from gout, arthritis and rheumatism. The leaves, which are high in vitamin C, can be sprinkled on foods, which help digestion. For an upset stomach, you can simply chew the leaves fresh.

The tannin in the leaves of this plant is very good for healing mouth ulcers as well. Crush a teaspoon of fresh leaves in a mortar and pack into the mouth at the location of the sore and leave for twenty minutes. Repeat three times a day.

 ## OTHER USES

An infusion of salad burnet is used to refine and soften the skin and makes a good sunburn lotion. It's wonderful in a facial steam or facial pack as well. To freshen stale air, make a strong tea of burnet and mint leaves. Steep over-night and then strain the mixture through cheesecloth into a spray bottle. To use this herbal water, spray in a fine mist in rooms with a harsh or musty odor. This is great water to take on an airplane where the recycled air is dry and stale. I also use it in my car, right from the refrigerator, to stay awake and alert if I have to do a lot of driving. A mist or two in the face has probably saved me from several accidents.

 ## CULINARY USES

Before we had supermarkets, salad burnet was grown in many gardens as a staple for green salads, especially during the winter. The nutty, cucumber flavor in dishes is a real treat instead of the vegetable cucumber that can become watery. Three tablespoons of fresh, chopped leaves equal a half-cup chopped cucumber. Try burnet leaves in coleslaw, as well as green salads.

Fresh leaves can also be used in chilled molds, aspics, wine cups and other beverages like tomato juice. I use it in gazpacho, along with cucumber for a first course on a hot summer day. Add burnet, in addition to snipped dill and yogurt, to sliced cooked beets. Place leaves and lemon slices inside game hens before roasting. Remove leaves before serving. Use on sandwiches instead of lettuce, like you might watercress. I like it especially with tuna or avocados. For sandwiches on buttered brown bread, lay whole leaves pulled from the stalks. Leaves may be chopped, but it isn't necessary since they are small and soft. Use snipped leaves in cream cheese, dips, as a garnish instead of parsley, in French dressing, and mayonnaise purchased or homemade.

This herb blends very well with dill, basil, thyme, garlic, oregano, marjoram, and tarragon as well as a variety of lemony herbs. Borage and burnet leaves may be used interchangeably. Try burnet in fiery type dishes like Thai foods, curry, and salsa.

 ## RECIPES

White Wine Cup with Salad Burnet
(This is a lovely recipe to serve at a bridal shower.)

2 bottles dry white wine
1 cup brandy
1 cup black currant juice
12 oz. soda water
Handful of salad burnet leaves
12 strawberries

Mix all ingredients together in a large serving bowl, chill. Add ice cubes before serving.

Honeydew Melon with Salad Burnet and Ham
(Serves 6) This makes a cool first course for hot weather.

1 honeydew melon, cut into six slices and peeled (Other suitable fresh fruits may be substituted, such as casaba melon, cantaloupe or ripe pears.)
6 lettuce leaves, washed and dried
6 thin slices ham (preferably smoked or Proscuitto)
Few sprays of salad burnet

Arrange the lettuce leaves and the melon segments on six small
plates with the ham slices. Pull the burnet leaves from the stem
and scatter about a dozen over each melon slice. Serve chilled with
French dressing and freshly ground pepper.

Salad Burnet Soufflé

3 Tbs. butter
2 Tbs. flour
1 scant cup milk
Salt and pepper
½ tsp. Dijon mustard
½ cup Gruyere cheese
1 Tbs. chopped burnet leaves
3 egg yolks, lightly beaten
4 egg whites, stiffly beaten

Melt the butter in a saucepan, stir in the flour, and cook over a low
heat for one minute, stirring until smooth. Heat the milk and add
it to the pan. Continue to cook over a low heat, stirring constantly,
until the ingredients have blended into a smooth creamy sauce.
Simmer gently for three minutes. Add salt and pepper to taste.
Stir in mustard, cheese, and burnet leaves. Take off the heat and
cool for a moment, and then stir in the lightly-beaten egg yolks.
Cool for five minutes then fold in stiffly-beaten whites. Turn out
into a buttered 3-¾ cup soufflé dish and bake for 20 minutes at
400° F. Serve immediately.

Cabbage Slaw

½ lb. green cabbage, thinly sliced
½ lb. red cabbage, thinly sliced
10 green scallions, sliced with some of the green
½ cup chopped salad burnet leaves
¼ cup sugar
½ cup salad burnet vinegar
1 ½ tsp. whole celery seed
1 ½ tsp. dry mustard
1 tsp. salt
⅔ cup olive oil
Freshly ground black pepper

Place cabbages, onions, and burnet leaves in a large bowl. In a small saucepan, heat the sugar, vinegar, celery seed, mustard and salt to a boil. Boil two minutes until sugar is dissolved. Cool, then add olive oil and pour over mixed vegetables. Add pepper to taste. Toss well and chill thoroughly. Keeps for up to a week.

Salad Burnet Vinegar
Sterilize a glass bottle or jar and use about two cups of washed and dried fresh herbs, both leaves and stems. Add your herbs to the container with garlic or garlic chives or chive flowers. Then fill the jar with two to three cups of warmed red or white wine vinegar. Cover tightly with a cork and place in a cool dark place for a minimum of six weeks - longer for a more robust flavor. Strain through a fine mesh strainer, cheesecloth or a coffee filter, then transfer the vinegar to a sterilized jar or bottle and add new fresh leafy stems. Close with a cork.

Salad Burnet Skin Toner
(This toner softens and improves texture of oily skin.)

2 cups warmed white wine vinegar (witch hazel can be used as a substitute.)
½ to ¾ cup salad burnet leaves and stems

Add the burnet leaves and stems to the vinegar in a sterilized jar or bottle. Cap it tightly and refrigerate for two weeks. To use, simply dampen a cotton ball in water and then dampen with the vinegar mix.

Dab onto your face with a cotton ball after cleaning thoroughly. I do not rinse it off and the mixture does not need further refrigeration.

Facial Pack
(An herbal facial pack always has a liquid, solid and herb.)

2 Tbs. chopped burnet leaves
1 cup of boiling water
1 Tbs. powdered brewer's yeast
½ tsp. wheat germ oil
2 Tbs. strong infusion of salad burnet

Make an infusion with the burnet leaves and water and steep for ten minutes; partially cool. Blend together the yeast, wheat germ oil and infusion. While still warm, spread the mixture over your face. Leave it on for 10-15 minutes. Rinse your face in clear water and moisturize your skin.

Sunburn Lotion
(This lotion is not meant to act as a sunscreen, but rather as a skin lotion for use after getting too much sun.)

Warm one-quarter cup of mineral oil. Steep two tablespoons of chopped burnet leaves in the oil for two to three days. Strain out the leaves. Dab on skin with a clean cotton ball.

 **OTHER NOTES** _____

Thomas Jefferson covered sixteen of his acres with salad burnet as erosion control. He also used this area to graze livestock. Fields of burnet are used as animal forage in California and New Jersey. Sheep and game birds prefer it to clover. Like mint and thyme, burnet smells good when stepped or walked upon. A ground cover can be planted by using first-year burnet plants of six inches in height.

Salad burnet is stunning in the garden when teamed with lavender-cotton, rue, lady's mantle, or curry plant. Because of its high tannin content, the root of greater burnet can be used in the tanning of leather.

SAVORY

Winter & Summer Or Any Season

SAVORY

An old charm states: "Summer savory, I need you for my beans;
I plant when the moon is heavy, with marigolds in between."
Savory adds interest and spiciness to otherwise bland foods, and
its most common use is in cooking. Savory is known as the "herb
of happiness."

 ## BOTANICAL NAME _____

Savories are members of the genus, *Satureja*, that comprise about 30
species. This name is a derivative of the word for *'satyr,'* the half-
man, half-goat creature that roamed the ancient mythological
forests. According to legend, the savories belonged to the satyrs.
From the Latin, the word *'saatur'* means full. These plants are
members of the *Lamiaceae* family whose members are especially
notable for their pungency.

Summer Savory – <u>*Satureja hortensis*</u> – is also known as 'bean herb.'
A new standard summer savory called *'Aromata'* has more intense
aroma and peppery taste than older varieties. These dark green-to-
purple oblong and pointed leaves have a higher essential oil
content in a sturdier, shorter plant. In summer, the plant produces
small white-mauve flowers that are very tasty in several recipes.
Summer savory likes a planting bed of rich, light soil and lots of
sun. This annual grows from just 10-12 inches and the delicate
flavor is generally preferred over the more pungent winter savory.
This variety is sometimes considered a half-hardy annual because
it can withstand winters in milder climates.

Winter Savory – <u>*Satureja montana*</u> – is also known as mountain
savory and is a semi-evergreen shrub. This aromatic perennial has
erect stems with stiff branches growing to about 12 inches in height
and width. The dark green, narrow, oblong leaves are pointed, and
grow on all four sides of the stems; the pale purple or bluish-purple
flowers bloom in June. Winter savory has a sharper, spicier taste

than summer savory but is used for medicinal and culinary purposes in much the same way. It is woody, unlike the annual, but is easy to grow from seed; alternatively, it can be grown from root divisions or cuttings. This perennial cousin to the summer savory is an attractive low bush for borders and edgings.

Creeping Savory – _S. spicigera_ or _S. repanda_ – looks like a prostrate version of white-flowering winter savory. Its creeping habit makes it ideal for rock gardens and edgings. Standing just three inches tall with a spread of twelve inches, its masses of small white flowers appear in summer. This is a very attractive plant with glossy green leaves whose taste is not as hot as winter savory. It is native to southwest Asia and is hardy to zone 7. This is a rare perennial.

Lemon Savory – _S. biflora_ – is a sensational new savory from South Africa and South America. This tender perennial is remarkable for its intense lemon scent and flavor. Totally unlike other savories, it's easy to grow in well-drained soil and needs only occasional trimming. It has small white flowers and rounded leaves with a heavy lemon scent. It's used in tea and for flavoring fish and poultry.

Yerba Buena – _S. douglasii_ – means 'good herb' in Spanish. Of course, there are other herbs that the Spanish commonly call yerba buena, including many mints, also of the _Lamiaceae_ family. This evergreen, creeping, perennial trailer with rounded menthol-scented leaves on stems to two feet has white-to-purple flowers. It is native to the woodlands of western North America from British Columbia to California and is hardy to zone 8. When growing well, it reminds me of our native Twinflower, _Linnaea borealis_, trailing or prostrate rosemary in appearance. It makes a good houseplant or can hang in a basket.

Purple Flowered Savory – _S. coerulea_ – is a semi-evergreen, hardy perennial. Its height is 12 inches with a spread of eight inches. Its small purple flowers bloom in summer.

Pink Savory – _S. thymbra_ – is a Mediterranean herb growing to 12 inches with pink flowers. This variety was used to cleanse and freshen wine barrels.

HISTORY _____

Summer savory is native to southern Europe and the basin of the Mediterranean, while winter savory with the species name montana implies growth in the mountains of southern Europe and North Africa.

Ancient Egyptians used it in love potions and the Saxons named it savory for its spicy, pungent taste. This plant was used in medieval times to help spice up the starchy plain foods of the poor as well as to add a robust tang to the meatier diet of the rich. Culpeper stated that savory is good for 'affections of the breast,' and that 'it expels tough phlegm from the chest and lungs.' It was not actually cultivated until the ninth century, but the Italians may have been among the first to grow annual savory as a kitchen herb, and it is still used extensively in their cooking

The Romans introduced Britons to savory and it quickly became popular both as a medicine and a cooking herb. The Romans added it to sauces and vinegar, which they used liberally as flavoring as we use pepper today. In Northern Europe, it became an invaluable disinfectant as a strewing herb to ward off insects. In France, savory is known as garlic pepper or donkey's pepper because of its tartness. Winter savory was used to decrease the sex drive and summer savory to enhance it. Guess which variety the French prefer? The summer savory, of course! European trade brought savories to the New World as it was among the first herbs brought here by the Pilgrim Fathers. It is now naturalized in North America. It has been used to enhance the flavor of food for over 2,000 years.

In Germany, savory is known as pepper or bohnen-kraut, and in Holland as boonen kruid, both meaning bean herb. It does make an especially good companion to green beans and lentils. This herb is less in demand in America than in many other areas of the world. I think the American culture has not yet discovered its use for dissipating stomach gas.

TYPE

Summer savory is usually considered an annual, but in some climates can be grown year around as a semi-hardy annual. Winter savory is a hardy perennial in all of the climates where it grows.

DESCRIPTION

Summer savory has a modest but pleasant appearance and can be used as an annual ornamental plant. Its branching root system and bushy, fine hairy reddish stems, which tend to droop slightly, make it distinctive in any summer garden. The entire plant is highly aromatic and perfect for seasoning beans and squash. This almost miniature herb is a slender annual growing from 10 to 12 inches tall with leaves of soft green tinged to red. The leaves are spaced widely apart, lance-shaped, soft, hairless, linear, about one inch long and attached directly to the stem in pairs. The grayish leaves turn to a purplish color in late summer or early autumn. The tiny blue and white-to-lavender flowers appear three months after planting and last until frost.

Winter savory is a hardy semi-evergreen perennial bush about 12 inches high and 12 inches wide with woody stems at the base. It has a heavier aroma than summer savory, which is sweeter and more delicate. The narrow, firm, shiny green leaves are similar to summer savory but thicker. White-to-pink flowers are smaller and bloom from mid-season until frost; they are grouped in terminal spikes. These leaves and flowers have a stronger, biting flavor than summer savory; therefore, they make a good pepper substitute. The plant is well shaped and decorates the permanent garden, especially when covered with diminutive plumes of snow-white blossoms, which appear in summer and fall. Here the bees hover for hours at a time. Even when I cut a few branches for flavoring, the bees don't seem to notice me, as they are so intent on gathering the fragrant nectar.

There is a lesser known form of winter savory, *S. montana* subspecies *illyrica*, whose leaves are a little smaller and more lush, with white flowers more thickly clustered than those of upright savory. It spreads in dense cushiony mounds, making a very attractive plant for borders or for filling pockets in rustic paved paths, terraces, and in dry stone walls. Cut back this prostrate variety hard when cold weather starts, and it will reward you by flourishing even more the following summer

 # PLANTING & CARE REQUIREMENTS __

All savories like to grow in well-drained, light soil in a sunny, sheltered position. Use fresh seed, as its viability decreases rapidly. Summer savory can be started from these fresh seeds in flats in a light, rich soil and planted in April. Transplant when the weather is quite warm and the plants are four-to-six inches tall. If grown indoors, transplant outdoors after hardening them off for a few days. Summer savory also grows well from seed sown directly in the ground in late spring or when there is no danger of cold temperatures and the ground can be worked. Germination and growth are rapid whether sown one-quarter inch deep outdoors or indoors in flats six weeks before the expected date of the last frost. Thin the plants to six inches apart, give them some light fertilizer, and keep well-weeded. After the first light feeding of fertilizer, withhold further fertilization or the plants will keel over. When the seed is sown early in spring, the plant is ready to pick at the beginning of summer. It is a good strategy to have successive sowings of savory seed well into the middle of summer for a continuous fresh crop. Harvesting then can continue until late autumn.

After some growth has occurred, mound soil slightly around the bases if plants start to flop. Summer savory plants left to flower will set seed and usually volunteer new plants in the spring. In hotter climates, savory flowers and goes to seed while plants are still small.

Winter savory can be started from seeds sown six-to-eight weeks before the last spring frost, but is best propagated from cuttings or layering. Lightly press seeds into a starter mix but do not cover, as they need light to germinate. When they grow a few inches tall set them in the garden 10-12 inches apart after the soil has warmed up.

The winter savory will grow into a decent-sized shrub if the conditions are right. Give it a moderately rich, sandy soil with a good supply of moisture for the seedlings. It prefers full sun, good drainage, and a ph of 6.5 to 7 is optimum. It's easier to start winter savory from three-inch potted plants because they are so slow growing; on the other hand, they are hardy and will grow almost anywhere. A plant in full sun will produce fine growth if the roots are kept moist and the leaves dry. Keep the plant clipped to induce new growth. Winter savory makes a nice low border or edging plant. Although it looks pretty in the summer, it can look a bit sparse in the winter months. Again, trim it from time to time to maintain shape and promote new growth. Winter savory is hardy as far north as New York City but is a short-lived perennial and will probably need to be replaced with new plants every two or three years from seeds, cuttings, or divisions.

Summer savory also makes a good subject for an indoor container garden but bring it inside for the winter if you live in a cold climate. Indoors, plant savory in a wide pot so the roots have plenty of room. It needs six hours of sun per day. It grows in any well-drained soil of average-to-poor fertility. Summer savory planted out in the garden will die in winter.

Creeping savory does not like cold wet winters or, for that matter, clay soils. Plant in a sunny rockery or a well-drained sheltered corner. As a strong aromatic plant, savory is mainly free from pests and disease. It grows nicely in containers if lightweight, fast-draining potting soil is used. In the Pacific Northwest, with our rainy winters and clay soil, planting a potted creeping savory is the only way to grow this delightful plant successfully.

The essential oils in savory are similar to thyme and oregano, and they make good companion plantings.

HARVESTING

When picking winter savory, several inches of the tender tops are the most satisfactory. Cut winter savory back often in early summer to stimulate young tender growth. It takes a while for new growth to mature and harden off before winter. The taste is milder then, more like the lighter taste of summer savory, while mature leaves are hotter.

Pick the flowers as soon as they begin blossoming. The savories' nature, so sweet in the garden, becomes fierce when you try to strip the sharp-pointed leaves from the stems of the winter variety. If you're not wearing gloves, you will get pricked, but the effect is not long-lasting. In winter, the plant reduces to a much lower shrub and the leaves become quite unyielding. If using them green, chop them very finely. Winter savory can be harvested fresh all winter. When the leaves are dried, crumble winter savory very finely or grind it in a blender or spice grinder.

Both fresh and dried summer savory leaves are softer than winter savory. You can begin harvesting summer savory as soon as plants are about six inches tall. If you keep snipping the tops of the branches, you'll be able to extend the harvest and keep it from getting leggy. Continue harvesting so that the plant doesn't flower, and this will maintain its flavor. Once summer savory flowers, pull up the entire plant and dry it. You can actually get several harvests during the growing season plus a final harvest before frost for summer savory.

PRESERVATION

Savories dry very well, retaining much of their essential oils. Harvesting of the herbs must be done when the weather is dry, as wet weather can be a problem. When plants insist on flowering, cut the whole plants. The woody stems can be removed from the leaves or you can dry whole stems with leaves attached. Cut the herbs early in the day once dew has evaporated and the plants are dry. It is important that contamination from animals, and gas or other fumes are avoided, as well as chemical crop sprays from a neighboring field. Snip the plants and place a single layer into a flat box or tray. If they are heaped up, they can deteriorate. When dry (in two days or so), strip the leaves from the stems and store in airtight jars. Both savories are best harvested just before flowering.

If you wish to dry plants by hanging them, gather together several stems, wrap with a rubber band and place a hook through the band. Hang upside down in a dry place out of the sun. Warmth, ventilation and shade are necessary for satisfactory drying. If you hang herb stems in bunches, keep them small so the center can dry quickly. If it takes too long to dry the center, outer leaves may become too brittle and crumble. A well-ventilated attic can be used for drying if it's not dusty; otherwise you need to place a paper bag over the herbs. Cut holes in the bags so that moisture can escape. Because the kitchen has dust, grease and cooking smells, this is not a good place to hang herbs to dry, especially near the stove. A cupboard can be used if there is good ventilation. I have used the top of my refrigerator with good results. The warmth of the motor creates enough heat and a covering of cheesecloth keeps the herbs clean.

When flowers are dry and papery, they have been properly dried. Stems of the herbs should snap easily and the fully dried leaves should readily part from the stems. You can test them by rubbing the sprig gently between the palms of the hands. Leaves should be brittle and aromatic, not brown and overdone, and should crumble. Placing some herbs in a tightly lidded glass jar and leaving them in a warm place for several hours can do a simple test for dryness. If there is the slightest sign of condensation on the glass, the drying process is not complete. After thoroughly dry, store the leaves and flowers whole in a sealed container in the dark. Light, heat, moisture and time destroy essential oils, so it is important to store your dried herbs in well-labeled, dated, airtight containers. Guard against mice, moths and insects because they love these aromatic plants.

Dried savory is usually readily available, but look for whole leaves rather than powdered ones. Once herbs have been crushed or powdered, they no longer contain the volatile oils that make them aromatic and flavorful. Cut only the quantity of material that you can dry at once. Once you cut the plants, you must dry them as soon as possible, as fresh-cut savory will quickly deteriorate.

Collect seeds as soon as they start to brown, place in an airtight jar with a desiccant added, and store in a cool, dry place. Seedpods should crack and crumble between fingernails.

Summer savory plants may be pulled up and dried in late summer. Later harvests of winter savory may be made throughout the summer and dried at any time.

 ## PROPAGATION

Winter and summer savory are easy to grow from seed or you may take cuttings of winter savory when it's over one year old. Soil layering can also propagate winter savory. As the seeds are tiny and difficult to collect, I prefer to buy a packet of seeds, which saves a lot of work. After sowing the seeds, leave them uncovered. They should germinate in about ten to fifteen days and be ready to harvest in sixty days. The germination rate is as high as 70 percent. Bottom heat is not necessary, so you don't need a greenhouse. When the seedlings are large enough and after a period of hardening off, they can be planted out into a prepared site in their permanent location. They will self-sow generously the next spring.

The bushy winter savory grows fairly slowly, supplying fewer leaves after two or three seasons. Roots can be divided in spring, as creeping savory stems have their own root systems with a root in each section similar to creeping thyme. Dig up an established plant in the spring after the frosts have finished and divide into as many segments as you require.

Prune winter savory plants in the spring and again in midsummer to maintain their shape. They should be replaced with new plants every three years. In the plant's third year, I simply lay a couple of the longest stems on the soil and cover them with about one-half inch of soil. I hold the stems to the soil with a large opened paper clip. New plants will be ready the next spring. I have a continuing supply of fresh savory using this method. For softwood cutting, remove several branches in the spring. Tuck them in sandy soil with some bark and potting soil and they will root. When these have rooted, plant them out 12 inches apart.

 MEDICINAL USES _____

The most well known medicinal use for savory is its effectiveness in relieving flatulence; the product Beano™ is very similar to savory. Savory has carminative, antispasmodic, and expectorant action. It is highly valued as a gargle for a sore throat as its essential oils include carvacol and thymol which have anti-fungal, antibacterial and antioxidant properties. Other active ingredients include p-cymene and tannin, which give it mild antiseptic and astringent properties. Its antiseptic properties have the power to ferment intestinal flora, thus soothing the stomach.

In Elizabethan times, the leaves were crushed into poultices for the treatment of colds and chest ailments like asthma. To alleviate chest colds, bring eight ounces of water to a boil in a saucepan and add one teaspoon of dried winter or summer savory (or one tablespoon fresh chopped). Cover and simmer for one minute. Turn the heat off and steep for several minutes longer. Strain and drink hot. Sweeten with a little honey if you desire; a few drops of lemon juice may be added too. A tea of savory is potent for diarrhea as well as indigestion but can also stimulate the appetite. Cherokee Indians used the herb as a snuff to cure headaches. It is even used as an aphrodisiac.

Fresh leaves rubbed on insect stings will relieve pain. The medicinal properties have also been valued for the treatment of colic, giddiness and respiratory troubles. A cloth soaked in savory tea helps relieve tired eyes.

Regarded as a promoter of regular menstruation, a savory tonic is good for the reproductive system. It was much commended for pregnant women to take internally as well as to inhale often.

The Germans first prescribed one cup of tea a day for diabetics, since savory contains anti-diuretic properties that can help keep them from having a dry mouth, a common symptom. This pleasant tasting tea is relatively harmless in moderate amounts.

 OTHER USES _____

I have used savory as the background on wreaths and used the dried plants for bouquets. Winter savory makes a handsome, dense edging plant for the front of the garden border and a good camouflage for woody, bare plant bases. It's very attractive spilling over and softening the hard edges of garden beds. The flowers can be made into an infusion for an antiseptic facial steam or added to the bath for oily skin. Its chemical properties act as an astringent. Its volatile oils are distilled in wines and spirits and the perfume industry.

 CULINARY USES _____

Savory is used commercially to flavor baked goods as well as liquors, bitters and vermouth. Romans used it in sauce and also in pies. With its distinctive peppery taste, savory is used in cooking to help digest many foods. It contains the volatile oil thymol (as does thyme) and tastes somewhat woodsy like thyme. While being stimulating and pleasing to the taste buds, savory is also an excellent substitute for pepper and other spices that do not agree with some people. Pork and cucumber, two dishes that are difficult to digest, are made easier with use of savory. It may be used to strengthen mild herbs or soften the effect of more robust herbs. Summer savory's flavor is reminiscent of aromatic marjoram and thyme together, a blend of sweet and spicy tastes; whereas winter savory has more peppery and piny tones, giving it a heartier character.

Summer savory is one of my favorite blending herbs as it contributes its mildly piquant taste to mixtures with parsley, bay, basil, marjoram, oregano, rosemary and thyme. Both summer and winter savories, often called the bean herb because of the compelling character, are added to a dish whose base is peas, beans or lentils. It also has an affinity with broccoli, brussel sprouts, potatoes, poultry, rabbit, and fish. Savory is also very good with meats, especially pork, beef and veal, and wonderful with corn. Only the winter and summer savories are generally used in cooking. The other varieties have an inferior flavor.

The peppery relish of savories not only gives beans a lift, but the herb may be mixed with bread crumbs for coating fish, pork, and veal fillets before frying or baking. It is an excellent herb in seafood sauces and cocktails, in lentil, pea and bean soups, and in soufflés. With cabbage, turnips, potato salad and tossed green salad it gives an unusual tang. Summer savory blends well with most flavors, helping to bring them together. This herb is popular in teas, herb butters, soups, eggs, snap beans, peas, rutabagas, eggplant, asparagus, parsnips, onions, squash, garlic, liver, and quince chutney. Savory offers a nice change to tomatoes rather than using basil, marjoram or oregano. It can be used in place of parsley and chives as well. Use it sparingly, however, until you are used to its culinary strength.

Savory and chive blossom vinegar is a wonderful combination, and savory adds depth to tofu dishes. Herb butters and oils are also good uses for this spicy herb. Chop savory along with marjoram and parsley for an omelet. Chopped savory is also excellent in chilled vegetable juices and meatloaf. Soften goat cheese and add chopped savory to spread on baguette slices. This is a good blending herb for multi-ingredient dishes and it's a major ingredient in salami. German cooking is famous for savory and beans, and there are many claims that savory is an anti-flatulent.

Savories offer so many virtues to the cook: versatility, affinity with other herbs, good flavor when dried and the bonus of being easy to grow. It is almost exclusively used in cooking today rather than for other uses.

 **RECIPES**

Since I discovered several years ago that savory prevents flatulence (gas) we now use many different bean recipes. We really love fresh and dried beans and legumes and they are very healthy and full of fiber.

Herbes de Provénce
Use equal amounts of fresh or dried savory, marjoram, thyme and lavender. This mixture can be used as a dry rub for meats, to flavor homemade pasta, or for vinaigrette.

Cheese Appetizer
Cut mozzarella cheese into small squares and dip each into beaten egg. Dredge the dipped squares in a mixture of breadcrumbs and minced, fresh savory. Bake at 450° F. until the cheese has just begun to melt and the crumbs have begun to crisp. Serve with tomato sauce that has been flavored with savory.

Baked Potato Skins
Cut baked russet potatoes into quarters lengthwise and scoop out the pulp. Save the pulp for another use. Sprinkle the quarters with grated cheddar and minced fresh savory and bake at 475° F. about 7 minutes or until cheese has melted.

Savory Mayonnaise
1 whole egg
¼ tsp. salt and a pinch of pepper
1 Tbs. Dijon mustard
2 Tbs. red wine vinegar
1 cup good olive oil
3 Tbs. fresh minced savory

Place egg, salt, mustard, vinegar, and dash of pepper in a blender or food processor and whirl for about ten seconds. With machine running, begin adding oil in a slow, steady stream for about one minute. At this point, mayonnaise should be thick and stand on its own. Remove from the blender and stir the savory in carefully. (This recipe is also great with tarragon.)

Winter Savory Vinaigrette
2 Tbs. fresh lemon juice
Salt and fresh ground black pepper
2 tsp. Dijon mustard
1 Tbs. chopped shallots
1 clove garlic, minced
1 Tbs. chopped fresh winter savory
6 Tbs. extra virgin olive oil

Stir together all but the olive oil. Whisk in the olive oil.

Savory Marinade
Mince fresh summer savory leaves and combine with garlic, bay, and lemon juice. Use as a marinade for fish.

Family Soup
(Serves 6)

1 lamb shank
1 ham hock
½ lb. beef stew meat, cut in chunks
1 carrot, peeled and diced
1 parsnip, peeled and diced
1 turnip, peeled and diced
2 stalks celery, chopped
2 onion, peeled and chopped
2 cloves garlic, peeled and left whole
8 oz. beans of your choice (navy, pinto, or red beans are my favorite)
8 oz. lentils (orange or brown)
Black peppercorns
3 bay leaves
4 Tbs. fresh savory stems (or 2 Tbs. dried)

Put all the ingredients together in a soup pot with enough water to cover (about 4 quarts). Bring to a boil, turn the heat down and simmer slowly for 2 ½ to 3 hours skimming off any foam. Before serving, lift out the bones. You can cool the soup to skim off any fat.

Tofu Eggs with Savory
(This is from my friend, Ruth Afflack, whose favorite herb is savory.)

Canola oil
½ cup tofu, cubed
¼ cup minced onion
2 eggs
¼ cup milk
2 tsp. dried savory (4 tsp. fresh)
½ cup spinach or ¼ cup peas, broccoli, or asparagus (optional)
¼ cup cheddar cheese

Saute' tofu and onion in the oil. Beat eggs and add the milk and savory. Add egg mixture and optional vegetable to tofu. Cook over medium heat. When the egg is about set, add the cheese. May be served on wheat toast.

Savory Corn Relish
(We like this on soft taco shells with ground meat. Makes six pints.)

24 ears fresh sweet corn, husked
2 ½ cups assorted sweet peppers, diced
2 cups onion, diced
1 ½ cups water
½ cup olive oil
½ cup honey
1 cup white *wine* vinegar
1 Tbs. pickling salt
2 tsp. celery seed
4 Tbs. winter savory, chopped
1 Tbs. yellow or brown mustard seed
3 garlic cloves, minced

¾ tsp. ground turmeric
6 winter savory sprigs

Bring a kettle of water to boil and cook 12 ears of corn for 3
minutes. Remove the corn, refresh in cold water and pat it dry.
Cook the remaining 12 ears in the same way. Cut the kernels from
the cob. There should be at least 10 cups of corn. An extra cup will
not affect the recipe. In a large pot, combine the peppers, onion,
water, olive oil, honey, vinegar, salt, celery seed, savory, mustard
seed and garlic. Bring these ingredients to a simmer and cook for 5
minutes. Add the corn and bring to a boil, reduce heat, and simmer
for about 5 minutes, stirring occasionally so that the relish does not
stick. Combine 2 Tbs. of the liquid with the turmeric in a small cup,
then add the mixture to the pot and stir well. Simmer 2 minutes
longer. Ladle the relish into 6 hot sterilized pint jars with a sprig of
savory in each jar. Seal the jars and process in boiling water for 15
minutes. Refrigerate any unsealed jars and use within a week or
two.

Prawns in Savory Yogurt Sauce
(Serves 2)

9 oz. natural, plain yogurt
1 ½ Tbs. tomato paste
2 tsp. finely chopped savory leaves and/or flowers
1 tsp. soy sauce
8 oz. prawns (cooked and peeled)

Mix all the ingredients together except the prawns. Chill the sauce.
Fold prawns into the sauce. Serve in individual glasses as for
prawn cocktail. An excellent accompaniment is a small plate of thin
brown bread sandwiches filled with chopped marjoram or parsley.

French Bread with Savory Topping
1 cup mayonnaise (above or regular)
¾ cup grated Parmesan or Romano cheese
½ cup chopped onions or scallions
1 tsp. Worcestershire sauce
2 Tbs. chopped summer savory
1 loaf French bread split in half lengthwise

Place topping ingredients in food processor and blend with 3-4 pulses. Spread half over each piece of bread and bake for 15-20 minutes in 350° F. oven.

Green Beans with Savory
1 lb. green beans, trimmed to 1 inch pieces
2 Tbs. butter
¼ cup grated Parmesan cheese
1 Tbs. finely chopped savory
Ground black pepper
Fresh lemon juice

Steam beans in a saucepan for 5 minutes. Melt butter in saucepan and add cheese and savory and mix together. Season with pepper and lemon juice. Toss beans in mixture until they are coated. You won't miss salt with this excellent savory flavor.

Baked Beans with Savory and Sage
7 cups hot water
2 cups dried small white beans (about 1 lb.)
½ cup yellow onion, chopped
2 Tbs. olive oil
5 fresh sage leaves
1 ½ tsp. finely chopped fresh summer savory or 1 tsp. winter savory
1 large clove garlic, minced
2 tsp. Dijon mustard
Salt and ground black pepper
Paprika

In a 3-quart saucepan, bring hot water to a boil. Add the beans, reduce the heat to very low, cover and simmer very gently for 1 to 1-½ hours, or until beans are tender (keep beans covered with water). In a small skillet over low heat, gently saute' the onion in the olive oil for 4-5 minutes. Remove from heat. Drain beans in a colander but reserve the liquid. Place the beans into a large bowl and add the sauteéd onion, sage, savory, garlic and mustard. Stir to combine and season with salt and pepper. Transfer the bean mixture to a 2-quart casserole or bean pot. Add enough of the reserved bean liquid to cover the beans by one-half inch (add hot water as necessary to keep beans covered). Sprinkle top with paprika. Bake in 325° F. oven and bake for 2 to 2-½ hours or until most liquid is absorbed and top starts to brown. Beans should be moist but not too mushy. Remove sage leaves before serving.

Couscous with Mushrooms and Savory
2 cups vegetable stock or defatted chicken stock
1 cup of couscous, white or whole wheat
1 bay leaf
1 Tbs. olive oil
1 clove garlic, minced
7 oz. Swiss chard or other greens, chopped
8 large fresh mixed wild mushrooms
1 Tbs. minced fresh savory
1 tsp. balsamic vinegar
Black pepper
Parmesan cheese

In a medium saucepan, bring the stock to a boil. Stir in the couscous and bay leaf, cover, and remove from the heat. The couscous will absorb the stock while you prepare the rest of the dish. Heat a large saute' pan over high heat, and then pour in the oil. Reduce the heat to medium, add the garlic, greens, and mushrooms, and saute' until the greens are not quite wilted, about 2 minutes. Add the savory and saute' another minute until the mushrooms are cooked through. Add the vinegar and toss until fragrant. Combine the greens mixture with couscous, adding pepper and cheese to taste. Serve as a vegetarian light entrœ'.

Oatcakes with Savory
4 cups rolled oats (not the instant kind)
1 tsp. salt
3 Tbs. butter or margarine
2 Tbs. chopped savory leaves and/or flowers
½ cup warm water

Place the first four ingredients in a bowl and mix by hand or in a food processor. Slowly add warm water until dough forms a sticky ball. Roll out on a floured board to one-eighth inch thick. Cut in rounds and place on ungreased cookie sheet. Prick the round and bake in a medium oven 15-20 minutes until light brown.

Pork Chops and Apples with Savory

2 medium onions, chopped
4 Tbs. vegetable oil
3 tart apples, peeled, cored and sliced
4 6-oz. pork chops, 1 inch thick
2 Tbs. flour
3 Tbs. brown sugar
1 Tbs. chopped winter or summer savory
1 ½ cups defatted chicken stock or water
Ground black pepper

Sauté onions in oil for 5 minutes, then remove from skillet and set aside. Sauté apples in same skillet for 5 minutes; remove and set aside. Dust pork chops with flour and sauté in the pan for 3 minutes per side until lightly browned. Add extra oil to skillet if needed. Sprinkle sugar and savory on top of each pork chop then cover with onion and apple slices. Season with pepper. Add liquid to the skillet and simmer over medium low heat for 20-25 minutes. Sauce will thicken.

Savory Sausage

1 lb. ground pork (I grind my own in my food processor from pork butt, trimmed)
1 lb. ground veal or beef (I grind my own, trimmed)
½ small onion
2 cloves garlic, minced
1 ½ Tbs. minced winter savory or 2 tsp. dried winter savory
¾ tsp. allspice
1 tsp. salt
¼ cup dry white wine
Pepper
Pinch ground cloves

Wet hands, place meats in a large bowl and mix together. Blend in the onion, garlic, savory, allspice, salt, white wine, pepper and cloves. The sausage should be well seasoned. Check by frying about a tablespoon of the mixture; taste and adjust the seasoning. If you ground your own meat and therefore have made it less fatty than the commercial variety, it may tend to stick, just add a tablespoon of olive oil to the meat mixture. Stuff the sausage into casings (from the butcher) or wrap tightly and store in the refrigerator. Let the sausages season for a day or two before cooking or you may freeze it for a few weeks. Brown in pan heated to medium and add a little water.

OTHER NOTES

Savory is a popular herb to grow near beehives because of the pleasant-tasting honey it produces. Winter savory shrubs made popular hedges in Tudor herb and knot gardens and in shrub mazes. Both savories have a history of regulating sex drive. Winter savory was thought to decrease sexual desire, while summer savory was said to be an aphrodisiac. Naturally, summer savory became the more popular of the two. The Egyptians used it in a popular love potion. The French sipped savory mixed with wine as a love potion for both sexes. In England, savory was mixed with beeswax and used as a back massage lotion for unromantic women. (I wonder if that worked?) Once the colonists brought the herb to America, however, its romance ended.

In the Middle Ages, a garland fashioned of savory leaves and flowers was worn as a crown or cap to revive the wearer from drowsiness. High in vitamin A and calcium, savory also contains niacin, iron and potassium.

NOTES

SORREL
The Tart Salad Herb

SORREL

The first green to appear in my spring herb garden is young fresh sorrel. Frenchmen for centuries have prepared spring cream-of-sorrel soup to quicken the blood and enliven the appetite. This plant, sometimes considered a vegetable, is becoming one of the herbs most in demand in America after being little used in the past.

 ## BOTANICAL NAME

The generic name, *Rumex*, comes from the Latin rumo, "I suck." The name, sorrel, however, is from the Old French word surelle, meaning, "sour." Other names include green sauce, sour dock, cuckoo sorrow or cuckoo's meat. All of the names refer to its tangy sour-like taste. It really is very good, though! It is a member of the buckwheat or *Polygonaceae* family. There are more than 100 species in the *Rumex* genus and many of them are certainly considered weeds.

Common Garden or Wild Sorrel – <u>*Rumex acetosa*</u> – is an erect perennial native to Europe and parts of Asia, growing wild in woods and meadows in North America and Greenland. It grows into a robust clump of foliage with deep roots. The 5-inch long lance-shaped leaves look like arrowheads. Its branching 3-foot flower-stalks have hundreds of greenish-brown flowers in summer that would be quite inconspicuous if there weren't so many of them. As the flowers ripen into fruits they turn a reddish-brown. This variety with the larger and tender leaves has a mild flavor and reminds me of bright lemons with its wonderful piquancy for soups, salad and sauces. The flavor is quite bland in the early spring but its acidity increases later on.

True French Sorrel – <u>*R. scutatus*</u> – also grows in clumps - much like spinach - about 6-inches tall with smooth, broad leaves and a refreshing acid taste. It grows on old walls and in mountain pastures in western Asia and North Africa. Its smaller size and shield-shaped leaves distinguish it from the common sorrel. The succulent leaf of this plant is the most fresh and lemony-tasting sorrel. Its small leaf makes a good ground cover and also looks good in pots. *Blonde De Lyon* is the standard variety esteemed in France. It prefers a warmer climate than what we can offer in the Pacific Northwest. The flavor of these leaves, although blander than *acetosa*, keeps a consistent taste throughout the season.

English Buckler Sorrel – *R. scutatus* '*Silver shield*' – has a decidedly silver cast to the mid-green leaves, which are shaped like squat shields with spreading stems. Although garden sorrel is much more commonly used for sorrel soup, these smaller buckler leaves are more concentrated in flavor and a little goes a long way. It also can be grown in window boxes. This sorrel is very similar to True French except that it is variegated in color.

Curled Dock – *R. crispus* – is an erect perennial, native to Europe and naturalized throughout the world. It was used by the Greeks in 500 B.C. It grows wild in wastelands and along roadsides as well as near sand dunes. Curled dock has long fleshy roots and branching stems reaching 2-4 feet. The large oval leaves have wavy edges and are tender in the spring but become bitter later in the season. The green flowers bloom from June to October. This herb, high in iron, is recognized medicinally as a tonic and prescribed for anemia and general debility. It has also been used as a laxative and diuretic.

Red-veined Dock – *R. sanguineus* var. *sanguinus* – is a very pretty herb and is used decoratively. The long pointed leaves have wavy edges, a center vein of deep red and similar red veins running throughout the leaves.

Indian Sorrel – *R. dentatus* – is used mainly as a medicinal herb. It has been an antidote for stinging nettle by rubbing fresh leaves on the affected area. The leaves are also used to treat eczema and the root has purgative properties similar to rhubarb.

Sheep Sorrel – *R. acetosella* – is native to central and southeastern Europe. It grows widely throughout the world except in tropical climates. It is much smaller than either common or French sorrel. It was traditionally used for fevers, inflammation, diarrhea, excessive menstruation and cancer. This is one of the four ingredients of the Essiac anti-cancer remedy. Although leaves are small and slow to gather, they are delicious to eat.

Wood Sorrel – _Oxalis acetosella_ – is a lively little clover-like herb. It contains too much oxalic acid to taste good but herbalists use the juice for stomach ailments. It can be very invasive by multiplying on underground runners. The mid-green leaves are shaped like a barbed spear. It grows wild on heaths and in grassy places. This is not a true sorrel but looks and tastes very similar to other sorrels.

 # HISTORY _____

The earliest known use of sorrel was in ancient Egypt and Rome where they nibbled on the leaves as an antidote to rich, decadent foods. It had both a soothing effect and was a digestive aid to relieve bloating. In Ireland it was popular served with fish and milk. In England, sorrel was common in sweet pastries and was used throughout Europe as a tonic against scurvy. Even though it wasn't known then that vitamin C could prevent scurvy, sorrel has a very high vitamin C content.

The plant is native to Europe and Asia but now has naturalized in many countries throughout the world on rich, damp, loamy, acid soils. In Europe sorrel was greatly anticipated in the spring as the first spring crop to arrive. They also used it in spring tonic. Frenchmen have a traditional and passionate love of sorrel, especially with fish as the first sorrel harvest comes at the beginning of the fishing season.

In North America, when a farmer became thirsty in the fields from the heat he (it was usually always a he), would pluck some wild sorrel and eat it. Our American version, wood sorrel, has been popular with foragers. It has a characteristic tangy flavor, but isn't related to the cultivated sorrels. We have known sorrel as salad and potherb for a long time; it has just not been widely used. When my

Mother, Pearl, comes to visit she spots the sorrel plants in my herb garden and always asks why I have that old weed in the garden. She grew up on a ranch in Eastern Washington where the plant grew wild and they all considered it a weed.

TYPE

Sorrel is a hardy perennial and is closely related to wild dock, which really is a weed. It can also be grown as an annual, but will stay green all winter in mild climates, though the growth is limited. It is hardy to zone 3.

DESCRIPTION

Varieties of this plant can reach a height of six inches to nearly four feet. They can grow up to four feet across if left in the ground for several years. They spread by underground creeping stems. The leaves can be fairly bright green to a dull green to streaked. The leaves are shaped liked arrows, or shields, or are long and pointed. Leaves appear on tall stems in dense clusters. The leaves are not as flavorful in the spring but develop their acidity as the season progresses. They produce tiny round greenish flowers in summer. It looks a bit weedy but is a noble plant with inimitable flavor.

Male and female flowers are usually on different plants. Usually two to three plants would suffice in a garden if you wish to eat sorrel about once a week.

Although each sorrel described above has its particular uses (and tastes) the buckler sorrel is my favorite. The garden sorrel has a stronger, sharper flavor. The lemony tartness of all sorrel leaves is a cross between lemon and pepper. The slightly sour flavor with a lemony zest sparks the palate and salads as no other herb does.

PLANTING & CARE REQUIREMENTS __

Sorrel grows best in full sun, in rich, well-drained soil, but will do moderately well in partial shade and less fertile soil. It grows nearly year-round in my garden and doesn't seem to be fussy about sun or shade, damp or dry soil. It does need some extra watering during July and August when there is almost a drought around here. Using abundant fertilizer (with fish emulsion), plants will produce leaves from early spring until late in the fall.

Seeds may be sown in the garden in late spring or autumn either in a prepared box or where the plants are to remain. When seedlings germinate and grow to a couple of inches, thin to a distance of 12-18 inches apart. The plant tends to run to seed quickly, so to keep the leaves fresh and succulent, remove flower heads as they appear. In very warm climates sorrel leaves tend to become bitter. Mulch will keep the soil cooler and once the season cools down, the flavor will improve. Sorrel produces some of the earliest greens of spring and the latest of fall. Although a bed of sorrel in the garden can last for a decade or more, I like to replace mine every four years to keep it from getting too woody. Slugs and occasionally leaf miners attack sorrel, but should cause no problems with established plants. Remove the affected leaves and put out traps for the slugs. If the slugs do get to your plants and really devour the leaves, just cut the plants to the ground and the sorrel will come right back.

Sorrel can't withstand severe winters, but may be placed in a pot and brought into the house to set on a sunny windowsill during the coldest months. French sorrel makes a good low-growing pot plant. Use potting soil and make sure the container has room for the plant to spread. Water well in the growing season and feed with liquid fertilizer. You usually need to grow your own sorrel because it is very difficult to find in the market.

HARVESTING

Harvest leaves beginning in the spring. Cut off side leaves until plants become well established. Later leaves can be cut completely, right above the crown to stimulate the plant production. Pick young leaves throughout the growing season for fresh use and for freezing.

Flower stalks, which emerge with the heat of the summer, should be removed whenever you harvest leaves. As the weather warms the leaves get a little tougher. In a hot summer, water regularly to keep the leaves succulent. On the other hand, if the weather is too cool, they lose much of their lemony taste.

PRESERVATION

Although you may get fresh sorrel year around, production really slows in the winter. If you harvest regularly from June to September, you should have plenty to preserve. I don't feel the leaves dry very well as they don't retain the sharp lemony flavor. You may dry leaves flat in a shady place, however, if you wish and then crumble them just before you use them.

The best preservation method is to blanch leaves and then freeze in airtight containers. Blanch in boiling water just for a minute and immediately place in a bowl of ice water. Squeeze all of the water from the leaves before packaging. Leaves may also be preserved in vinegar but the sorrel will have limited uses.

Another method used to preserve leaves was to cook them over a slow fire with salt and butter, until all moisture evaporated. When cool, the sorrel was pressed into pots. When quite cold, tepid melted butter was poured over the top and the pots were sealed down and kept in a dry place. Once opened, however, the contents would not keep for more than three weeks. I have never tried this but it seems as though the butter would not be an adequate preservative.

 # PROPAGATION

Sorrel is easily propagated by division or seeding. Start seeds indoors in containers in late March or direct-seed in fertile soil in mid-spring through July. Sow into prepared seed or plug trays, using potting soil and covering the seeds with perlite. Germination is fairly quick (10-20 days without extra heat). When the seedlings are large enough and the soil has started to warm up, plant out 12-18 inches apart. Small leaves will be ready to harvest after just 60 days. These transplants will take several weeks longer to produce than the divisions.

Plants do not spread, but rather clump. Clumps should be divided every three to four years in early spring just as new growth begins. They may also be divided in the autumn and replanted two feet apart. Plant in light shade and keep seed stalks cut to increase summer quality, but good leaves will reappear in the fall even if plants bolt.

 # MEDICINAL USES

The diuretic and cooling properties of this acidic and astringent herb has been used for many bodily complaints. It can be used to make a nourishing refreshing tea or a cooling drink, an old-country remedy for fevers. Sorrel is recommended as being good for the blood, especially in spring. It is considered to have blood-cleansing and blood-improving qualities similar to spinach, which improves the hemoglobin content of the blood. Eating spring sorrel, which they call sour dock, helps cure spring flu among the Eskimos. Sorrel is beneficial to the kidneys and aids the digestion. Navajo herbalists use an infusion for a mouthwash and sores in the mouth.

They would put leaves on mouth sores and then chew to release the juices. The antiseptic properties of the essential oil soothe, heal, and dry wounds and sores. A compress made of the leaves soothes sunburn as well as itchy skin, although it has been found that the leaf may cause dermatitis in some individuals. It has been prescribed externally for scabbing, ringworm and boils. Because of high vitamin C content, its cure for respiratory ailments is probably valid.

Care has to be taken that sorrel is not used in too great a quantity or too frequently. Its oxalic acid content may damage health if taken in excess. Very large doses are poisonous, causing severe kidney damage as well as stomach upset. The herb should not be used medicinally by those predisposed to rheumatism, arthritis, gout, kidney stones or gastric problems. High in oxalic acid, common sorrel should not be taken continuously as this can lead to the formation of small kidney stones of calcium oxalate.

 OTHER USES _____

The cut flower stalks and seed heads make great additions to dried floral arrangement. A compress or facial steam may be used for acne or other facial spots. One-half cup of sorrel has as much vitamin C as an orange.

 **CULINARY USES** _____

Sorrel has been used mostly in French cuisine but also occasionally in English, Jewish, Swiss and German cookbooks. Piquant, delicious soup made with sorrel is popular in France and was highly regarded in the time of Henry VIII. It is now commonly used in European cuisine but is just becoming popular with American cooks.

Young tender leaves of up to six inches are better eaten fresh while older larger leaves are generally used in cooking. The tender fresh

green leaves grow to about eight inches and have an intensely
lemony flavor. Because of its natural tang there is no need to use
salt in sorrel dishes. Its most noted uses are in soup and sauce but
there are many more uses for sorrel in an American kitchen, or any
other kitchen. Sorrel has a reputation for sharpening the appetite
and it is an excellent herb to experiment with because of its great
versatility. A pound of sorrel looks like enough to feed a
neighborhood but when sautéed, it quickly reduces to a smooth,
silken purée equal to about half a cup.

Sorrel often accompanies fish because its high content of oxalic acid
is believed to dissolve tiny fish bones. Blend this herb with cream
and butter, never olive or vegetable oil which doesn't enhance its
flavor. In France, they dip sorrel leaves in batter and deep fry. It is
also used in beignets, a deep-fried pastry. You might wish to mix
minced sorrel leaves with vinegar and sugar as a condiment for
cold meats and fish. Use young tender leaves on a tuna sandwich
instead of lettuce for a nice tang. This herb's pleasant sharpness is
especially good with eggs and omelets and when combined with
mayonnaise makes a great topping for vegetables or fish dishes.
Cooked dishes will need less salt when sorrel is used.

Use the tender leaves in fresh green salads. Used sparingly in this
way they give a wonderful flavor, but a full salad of sorrel leaves
would really make you pucker. These salads can be dressed with
less vinegar or lemon juice to compensate for the increased acidity.
For a cooling salad, tear up sorrel leaves and lettuce leaves and toss
together in a French dressing that has been sweetened slightly with
a little honey. Use only a stainless steel knife or your hands to cut
or break sorrel; otherwise, the sorrel and utensil will be stained
black. Don't use cast iron because it will create a metallic taste.
It is advisable not to cook sorrel in an aluminum saucepan; like
spinach, its acid content reacts to the aluminum and it becomes
harmful. The tart, lemony flavor of iced sorrel tea can really cool
down a body from the inside out on a hot day.

Try a handful of shredded sorrel stuffed inside a chicken or other
poultry before roasting. Sorrel is excellent sautéed in butter or
softened with cream and added to vegetable soup. Use sparingly in
soups, omelets, fish sauces, and with poultry and pork. It is useful
for tenderizing meat by wrapping it around steaks or adding

pounded leaves to a marinade. Cook like spinach, changing the cooking water once to reduce acidity.

A customary use for sorrel was in a sauce as accompaniment to omelets, cold meat and fish, as the flavor is of a similar tartness to applesauce. Try my sorrel purée recipe below. Other ways to try sorrel is with red beans, diced on pasta, or combined with dill, chives or watercress. Use with potatoes, peas, spinach and even strawberries. Since I really love sorrel with fish, especially salmon, I hope you will try both salmon and sorrel recipes below - I love them both, and the colors are wonderful.

 RECIPES _____

The lemony tartness of this herb really dresses up the flavor of fish or pasta dishes and creates a tart essence for otherwise bland food.

Sorrel Purée

I am big on making my own soup stocks, purées, pastes, pestos, etc. This is the one recipe I prefer to preserve my sorrel supply for winter's use. This can be added to soups, stews and cream sauces.

Wash 4 cups sorrel leaves (the newer, smaller leaves), snip off the stems and place in a non-aluminum saucepan. Place about 2 inches of water in the pan and bring to a boil. Steam for a few minutes (with reduced heat), until sorrel has softened. Drain, cool a little, and then puree in a food processor. Freeze the purée in ice cube trays.

Sorrel Sauce

Sorrel leaves, about 4 oz.
1 oz. butter
1 Tbs. flour
10 oz. chicken stock (unsalted)
Cream and egg yolks, optional

Wash and finely chop a bunch of young sorrel leaves. Melt butter or margarine in a stainless steel saucepan and gently cook the sorrel until soft. Blend in the flour and add the stock. Stir well until

thickened. For extra smoothness, you may add 1 Tbs. cream.
An egg yolk may be beaten into the sauce immediately when it
comes off the stove. Serve over poached fish, pasta or vegetable,
especially carrots and fennel bulb.

Carrot and Sorrel Juice

2 lb. carrots, washed
½ lb. sorrel leaves
1 Tbs. lemon juice

Put carrots and sorrel through a juicer according to instructions.
Add lemon juice and serve immediately or chill over ice.
This healthy drink is very high in vitamin C and A.

Creamy Sorrel Salad Dressing

½ cup washed sorrel leaves
¼ cup plain non-fat yogurt
¼ cup half & half
2 Tbs. cream cheese, softened
1 Tbs. fresh lemon juice

Put all ingredients in a blender or food processor and purée. Chill
in bowl in refrigerator until ready to serve. Toss with salad greens;
serve on tomato slices, with tuna or chicken salad.

Sorrel Soup

4 oz. butter or margarine
1 small bunch of sorrel, shredded or chiffonade
2 quarts water
1 lb. potato, washed, peeled and diced
Pepper to taste
2 egg yolks

Melt the butter in a stainless steel saucepan, stir in the shredded
sorrel and simmer until softened. Add the water and the diced
potatoes, and pepper. Bring to a boil, and then simmer with the lid
on for 1 hour. Press the soup through a sieve, or purée it in a
blender. Reheat in the saucepan. Blend a little of the hot liquid into
the beaten egg yolks, pour into the saucepan of soup and stir well,

but do not boil again. Chill. Serve with a spoonful of cream in each bowl, and chopped cress or parsley. Serve hot in winter.

Sorrel Omelet

Blanch a handful of sorrel. Fry gently in butter and add some raw parsley and a little cream. While this simmers, make an omelet in the usual way. Thicken the sorrel mixture with an extra egg yolk and pour it at once in the omelet. Fold and serve hot.

Salmon with Sorrel

(I have two different recipes I use for this and like them both.)

6 small shallots sautéed in 2 Tbs. butter (do not use cast iron or aluminum pan). Add 12 ounces of fresh sorrel, stemmed. Stir and cook until purée forms. Add one-half cup white wine and two-thirds cup fish or chicken stock and cook until reduced by half. Add two-thirds cup whipping cream (unwhipped). Cook until reduced by about one third. Season with pepper and keep warm while you broil four 7-ounce salmon steaks, about 5 minutes on each side. Place a salmon steak on top of the sauce to serve.

Salmon with Sorrel Mousse

Melt 2 Tbs. butter in a large saucepan over medium heat. Add 12 ounces of stemmed sorrel leaves and cook, stirring occasionally, until sorrel has darkened a little and reduced to a purée (about 10 minutes.) Melt another 2 Tbs. butter in a second large frying pan over medium-high heat. When butter foams add 1-½ pounds of salmon filet and 2 Tbs. white wine and cook until it is opaque, (8 minutes.) Place 2 egg whites and a pinch of salt in a bowl of a mixer and whisk until they are stiff. Bring sorrel to a boil over medium heat, remove from heat and add the egg whites, whisking. Return to the heat and bring to a boil. Season to taste. Serve sorrel mousse on plate with salmon filet and top with a little melted butter.

Pasta, Mushrooms and Fresh Sorrel

1 Tbs. olive oil
12 oz. mushrooms, sliced
2 cloves garlic, minced
1 medium onion, sliced
1 cup chopped tomatoes
6 cups hot cooked pasta (tubular type to hold all the yummy sauce)
½ cup minced, fresh sorrel leaves

Heat a large sauté pan over medium-high heat, and then pour in
the oil. Add the mushrooms, garlic, onion, and sauté for about 5
minutes. Be careful not to burn the garlic (it turns bitter). Stir in the
tomatoes and cook until saucy and fragrant, about 7 minutes.
In a large bowl, toss the pasta with the sauce and sorrel.

Lentil and Sorrel Salad

1 ½ cup small green lentils
1 small onion, diced finely
2-3 medium-sized ripe tomatoes
1 cup fresh shredded sorrel leaves
2-3 cooked new potatoes, diced
2 garlic cloves, minced
⅓ cup olive oil
3 oz. mild goat cheese or feta cheese
Juice of ½ lemon
Pepper

Rinse and pick over the lentils. Put them in a pan with water to
cover by ½ inch. Bring to a boil, and then reduce heat and simmer,
covered, until they are just tender, 20-30 minutes. When the lentils
are done, drain and spread them on a baking sheet and toss with
the olive oil. Let them cool slightly, and then stir in the onion,
tomatoes, garlic and potatoes. Season with lemon juice and pepper.
When the lentils are at room temperature, stir in the sorrel leaves
and crumble in the goat cheese. The flavor improves if the salad is
refrigerated for 3-4 hours, then brought to cool room temperature
before serving.

 **OTHER NOTES**

Sorrel is a good dye plant, of soft pink with alum mordant, red and gold with chrome, and dark green with iron to create a yellow dye. Juice from the leaf was used to remove rust, mold, and ink stains from linen, wicker and silver, well before the days of Clorox™.

Rumex acetosa and *R. scutatus* attract the American Copper, lustrous copper and purplish copper butterflies. Sorrel is rich in potassium as well as in vitamins A, B1 and C. Sorrel leaves wrapped around tough cuts of meat were used as a tenderizer.

NOTES _____

TARRAGON
The Chef's Delight

TARRAGON

Of the thousand or so herb species I have grown over the past twenty-five years, my favorite herb is tarragon. I even named my new puppy Miss Tarragon Peterson (see back cover) and we call her Tarra. She shares our love of herbs and munches them daily as her salad. The name tarragon is derived from the French *esdragon*, meaning "little dragon." The Latin name is *dracunculus* and in the diminutive, drace or dragon. Its dragon-like roots may strangle the plant if it is not divided often. This is one of the herbs most in demand throughout the world and is known chiefly as a culinary herb. Chefs delight when they have an abundant supply.

 BOTANICAL NAME _____

French Tarragon – <u>*Artemisia dracunculus*</u> – this is the true French Tarragon - sometimes called little dragon. Tarragon belongs to a group of two hundred genuses (see binomial nomenclature in the glossary) in this artemisia family. The family is made up of aromatic herbs, most of which are bitter as well. The artemisia name comes from the Greek goddess Artemus, known in Rome as Diana. They are all members of the largest plant family in the world, the *Compositae*, which includes such different-seeming plants as sunflower, chicory, tansy, lettuce and thistle. It is easy to grow and very hardy once established. Tarragon is a very fragrant culinary herb with lance-shaped leaves.

Russian Tarragon – <u>*A. d. 'Inodorus'*</u> – Although this tarragon is not a true "herbal," I have included it because some retail outlets sell it as French tarragon, and I want you to know the difference. I do not recommend this variety of tarragon for culinary purposes as it has coarser foliage and almost completely lacks the odor and pronounced anise flavor characteristic of the true French variety. It is sometimes called false dragon. It grows to four feet with a spread of eighteen inches and can be invasive. It is more vigorous in growth and weedy. Some nurseries sell this as French tarragon because it grows well from seed. (Look for the botanical name or rub some between your fingers. It should have a tart, camphoranise smell.) Russian tarragon has a more sour taste. The plant originated in Siberia, which explains why it is so hardy.

Mexican Tarragon – _Tagetes lucida_ – is also known as sweet marigold or Mexican marigold. This perennial member of the marigold genus resembles French tarragon in flavor, but is coarser and more pungent. This species has sweet-smelling leaves and flowers. In warm and humid areas where French tarragon will not grow, this is an excellent substitute. It also can be substituted when French tarragon is dormant. The leaves make a stimulating tea. Although the seeds are slow to germinate, once the plant grows it is a popular stand-in as a potted herb. It can grow to three feet tall and will release its pronounced aroma by just brushing the leaves.

 HISTORY

Tarragon is native to the Caspian Sea and Mediterranean-area countries, southern Europe and Asia. It was the favorite herb of Charlemagne and cultivated in the gardens of the Tudors. First-century naturalist Pliny thought tarragon prevented fatigue. Tarragon has been used in the Middle East since at least the thirteenth century. Throughout the Middle Ages, faithful believers placed tarragon in their shoes before setting out on pilgrimages. People didn't know then that it was anti-fungal, but it did prevent many stresses to the feet. Arab doctors used its pleasant flavor and numbing properties to mitigate the effects of swallowing bitter medicines. It has grown in gardens for almost two thousand years in the Mediterranean, and used for one thousand years before being introduced to Europe. Although not a visually stunning plant, tarragon was at one time restricted to the formal gardens of the European nobility; hence, it was considered a royal herb. King Louis XIV's gardener declared tarragon "one of the best finishers of flavor." It is said that King Henry VIII divorced Catherine of Aragon for her reckless use of tarragon. I wonder if that was because they didn't have much of it to squander or because overuse created too much fire in his food.

In Europe, its strongest adherents are cooks rather than herbalists and doctors. Europeans cultivated it in kitchen gardens in drier, warmer areas. England had tarragon imported by about the 1500's and Dutch colonists introduced it to America in the middle of the 1600's. Although Thomas Jefferson was an avid and accomplished gardener, he wrote in his journal of 50 years "tarragon failed."

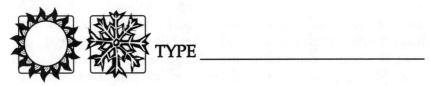 **TYPE** _____

Tarragon is a half-hardy perennial herb in our zones 7 and 8. But once established, it is a hardy perennial. It can stand a cold winter to -30° F if the soil doesn't hold moisture.

 **DESCRIPTION** _____

French tarragon has a rich, anise-like, peppery flavor and the complex aroma of a mixture of new-mown mint and licorice. It spreads into a bushy plant two to three feet tall. Its smooth olive-green, shiny, narrow leaves are about one to two inches long. The leaves are borne singly at the top of the plant in groups of three. The plant spreads by underground runners that are long, fibrous roots. Their slender branching shoots do not set seed. Growth is more lush in its second year.

Flower clusters are yellow or greenish-white, small, globe-shaped and quite inconspicuous. They rarely open fully, are usually sterile, and bloom from June to August in some climates. Erik Haakenson has what I considered a giant tarragon plant - over four feet tall - which he let me prune recently to preserve in vinegar. At first I thought it must be Russian tarragon at that height, but it was French tarragon. Leaves of Russian tarragon are lighter green and have star-shaped hairs. Its flavor is insignificant.

PLANTING & CARE REQUIREMENTS ___

Tarragon will thrive in a well-drained, sunny position in late spring, all summer, and will stay verdantly green through autumn. It withers away for a few weeks in winter. As soon as spring comes, the first shoots appear again. Tarragon most often fails from having been planted in wet or acid soil. It dislikes humid conditions. It needs well-drained loam or humus with sand. It is happiest in soil with a pH in the range of 4.9 to 7.5, but the optimum is 6.9. Though it likes full sun, it will grow well in partial shade if the roots are allowed to drain well. It can take up to thirty inches of rain a year, but will do fine on as little as eight inches. Do not allow plants to become stressed from lack of water during dry, hot summers. The plants become very sluggish in hot, humid weather. The fleshy roots, which resemble a tangle of snakes, are shallow and need some shade from hot summer sun. Place thick mulch over the roots in hotter climates. Roots need plenty of space to roam, as the plant grows from underground runners. If the climate is severely cold, give the roots some protection after the tops die back. Water only when the soil is completely dry. Tarragon hates soggy soil and will eventually tell you so by contracting root rot and flopping over dead. When my students and other clients ask me why their tarragon keeps dying, I tell them the usual reason is over-watering.

Plants should be spaced two feet apart and can be fertilized during the growing season twice a month, especially during the first few months after being transplanted. I use a 10-10-10 Alaska Fish™ liquid fertilizer diluted to half strength. I continue fertilizing throughout the early summer. Aged manure applied in early spring before growth commences will also give plants a needed boost. In late summer and early fall I fertilize just once a month until thirty days before night temperatures are expected to reach 40° F. In our climate in Washington state, that is early October. I stop fertilizing in the middle of September. Remove flowers in the summer. As the plant dies back into the ground in winter, it is an ideal candidate for either straw or deep mulch.

Although most herbs are sturdy and pest resistant, bugs, slugs, cutworms, and a variety of other little critters can bother them. Every spring in your herb garden, you can expect a few aphids, the usual crop of snails or slugs munching on tender greens and the occasional cutworm chewing off seedlings as they sprout. This is especially true of tarragon. Slugs love little tarragon plants. As soon as you see the plant peeking above ground, take measures to keep the critters away. Below I offer several ways that I have used to irradicate these pests.

Non-chemical controls are usually effective with these pests. Blast aphids off the plant with a spray of water or use Safer™ insecticidal soap. A mixture of garlic and water is also effective. Snails and slugs can be handpicked. Go out at dusk for a week or two and collect these pests in bags and put them in the trash. Place foil around the plant or use liquid slug bait. Placing four-inch high bands of copper (found in some nurseries) around susceptible plants or the whole planting bed is effective since slugs experience an electric shock when they slide their slimy bodies over the metal. To trap slugs, nail a couple of one-inch cleats to a board and place it cleat side down at the back of the bed. Check the underside of the board every morning and remove any slugs that have decided to make the protected board their temporary home. If I haven't remembered to put out boards, I sometimes skewer them with my barbecue skewers and then put them into a jar with ammonia water. As you can see, I have had years of experience trying to out-maneuver these pests. Most of these efforts will deter the critters.

White fly, spider mites and spittlebugs may be problems on tarragon, especially that grown indoors during winter. Spittlebugs can be felt in the middle of the foam they produce on the plant, but they shouldn't really hurt the plant. Several applications of Safer™ insecticidal soap controls spittlebugs, or a vigorous spray of plain water directed at the masses of foam from a hose nozzle works well. This is a cheap, effective, and environmentally sound way to rid plants of these pests. Repeat the treatment if new blobs of foam show up.

Microscopic roundworms or nematodes live beneath the soil and like sandy moist soil. They will suck moisture and nutrients from the plants, leaving stunted growth, and yellowing or wilting leaves. A soil sample needs to be taken and examined to determine if these pests are the cause, because chlorosis-withered or dying leaves may be symptoms of other problems. In any case, remove the damaged leaves. Some people suggest that mixing aged grass clippings into the soil prevents many of these bad nematodes. (There are also good nematodes that are very beneficial in the garden. These can be purchased through several gardening catalogues.)

Cutworms live in the soil and can shear off seedlings at ground level in a matter of minutes. Place a collar made from a four-inch section of paper toweling tube around each emerging plant

In late July and August, the plants can sustain fungus damage, which is evident by browning of the leaves. Check your plants occasionally for root rot or mildew, which are caused by fungus. Yellowish-brown to black roots and underground stems indicate root rot - too much water or poor drainage. Outer layers of roots slough off, leaving a central core.

Downy mildew and powdery mildew are a white, powdery mold on upper surfaces of leaves and petioles. Foliage wilts and browns, then drops. Remove diseased plants promptly. Prevention of fungus can be aided by circling plants with gravel or sand. This prevents water or mud containing the fungus from splashing on the plant.

With fungal or insect damage, leaves should be removed and the tops pinched to encourage new growth. Frequent harvesting of leaves, especially in summer, and a sand mulch lessen disease problems, but do remove all yellow or brown leaves as soon as they are observed to retard the spread of fungus. More tarragon is lost to fungus in temperate areas than from cold weather. Rust develops on French tarragon. When buying a plant, look for telltale signs of small rust spots - small orange raised spots - on the underside of a leaf. Discard any with rust.

Weeding should be done by hand and should be performed often so weeds do not crowd the plants. Mulch over the roots also helps to discourage weeds. Although tarragon is hardy to zone 4, the tops die back in freezing weather. Cut dead stems at ground level and apply a few inches of composted leaves or similar organic matter, if desired. The clump will always be larger in the second year, with shoots appearing in the late spring. If you grow healthy plants in the first place, keep them well weeded and welcome insect predators into the garden - bats, green lacewings and ladybugs - you will be well on your way to growing this magnificent herb. (See the glossary for other ideas of IPG - Integrated Pest Management.)

Tarragon grows well in containers. Use a soilless mix similar to Earthworks Herb Growing Medium™ or a bark and grit mix with potting soil. Since the plant produces root runners, give it room to grow so that it will not become pot-bound. Keep feeding potted tarragon to a minimum; overfeeding produces fleshy leaves with a poor flavor. You can bring it inside for a potted winter vacation, but it may transplant poorly if you return it to the outdoor garden. Tarragon takes special care indoors since it is essential for the plant to have a cold dormant period of at least three weeks. Indoor potted plants need dormancy and should be put in the refrigerator where temperatures average about 40° F. Plants should be cut back to about an inch high prior to refrigeration. After the cold period, plants should be grown under fluorescent lights about six inches above the plants. Light the plants for 16 hours a day. Research has shown that tarragon grows best during long days. Cold dormancy may also be done outside, but care must be taken not to let the plants get too cold, which kills the exposed roots. The dormant period may be anytime during the year if refrigeration is used, making it possible to stagger production with several plants and provide fresh tarragon year-round.

Tarragon dies back to the ground each winter even in mild climates; in cold climates, it should be well protected with mulch. If grown outdoors during the winter in a container, choose a wide pot with good drainage and do not overwater, especially during short winter days when the plants are not actively growing. Keep

the soil dry and the container in a cool, frost-free environment.
Divide and replant in fresh soil every spring and rotate plants
every three years.

After reading this section, you probably feel that growing tarragon
is not worth the effort, but if you provide good drainage, loose soil,
remove diseased plants promptly, and have thorough fall cleanup,
you will be successful. It has taken me many years with tarragon to
finally get it right.

 HARVESTING

Cutting stems often encourages branching, gives good air
circulation and prevents disease. If not picked regularly, stems
grow weaker and have a tendency to weep and mat on the ground.
In large shrubby plants, the stems should be harvested from the
center to open it up. Leaves may be picked anytime during the
growing season, but the most flavorful anise taste and largest
foliage occur in the spring, making the early season crop the best
for harvesting. Leaves may be harvested when stems are eight to
ten inches long. Cut the stems halfway down and they will quickly
branch with more large, tasty leaves. Two harvests can generally be
made each year, the first six to eight weeks after setting the plants
out and the second in mid-summer. When harvesting, handle the
leaves gently as they bruise easily. Any flowers they produce
should be removed to keep the plant productive. As the summer
warms, tarragon wearies, the diameter of the stems shrink, and
leaves become tiny shadows of earlier growth.

Cut down outdoor plants in late autumn and protect from frost by
covering them with leaves or straw.

PRESERVATION

The very best method of preserving tarragon is in white wine vinegar; the flavor is true and long lasting. Steep the leaves in warmed vinegar and place on a shelf for several weeks or months. This method retains much of its flavor and you can use the vinegar as well. To remove the vinegar taste from the tarragon, gently rinse it in cool water before using.

Although preserving in vinegar is the superior method for keeping tarragon, freezing the leaves can also be done. It is best to pick leaves in the early-summer months when flavor is at its best. Pick the tarragon leaves from the stem after rinsing with cold water and gently pat dry before freezing, being careful not to bruise the leaves. Some people advocate blanching the stems for thirty seconds and then plunging in ice water for two minutes. Put small amounts into labeled plastic freezer bags, either singly or in a mixture for bouquet garni. Place zip-lock bags in the freezer. When using these frozen herbs, crush in the bag while still frozen and add to recipe.

To dry tarragon, place sprigs on mesh screen in a shady but warm place. Drying emphasizes the hay aroma and licorice taste at the expense of the more volatile oils. The dried herb will not be as rich in flavor as fresh leaves. You may also hang the plants upside down in bunches in a warm, dry place out of the sun. They will brown somewhat in drying. Strip the leaves and pack into airtight containers for winter use. These dried leaves are a poor imitation of fresh tarragon. They seem to lose much of the complex flavors, and texture and color are not the same as the fresh herb. Dried tarragon can also be difficult to crush completely, so finely crush using a rolling pin before adding to a recipe. Use the same amount preserved herb as fresh rather than the usual one-to-three portions. (Generally three times more fresh herbs are used as dried ones.)

 PROPAGATION _____

Most gardeners acquire tarragon as seedlings, divisions, or cuttings. The tarragon seed that is sold to the unsuspecting public as French tarragon is nearly always that of Russian tarragon. So buyer beware. French tarragon looks as if it is going to flower, but the tight little yellowish buds rarely mature into blossoms, so seed of *Artemisia dracunculus* is virtually unobtainable and not viable.

As tarragon does not set seed in temperate climates, propagate by taking cuttings of rooted shoots. See the lemon verbena chapter for a description of taking cuttings. Start by growing three or four plants set twelve inches apart in spring.

To ensure the most flavorful tarragon, roots of established plants should be divided every two to three years in the spring, before new growth is three inches tall. Even in warm climates, the plants should be lifted and divided every two to three years to assure vigor and flavor. Dig up a plant and carefully separate it into pieces by pulling the roots apart. Each part will have some of last year's stem and roots. You will notice growing nodules that will reproduce in the coming season. Place a small amount of root, three to four inches in length and with a growing nodule, in a three-inch pot and cover with soil. Use a bark, grit and peat mix and place in a warm, well-ventilated place. Keep watering to a minimum. When well rooted, plant out in the garden after hardening off. Any extra clippings will be greatly appreciated by gardening friends who like to cook.

Softwood cuttings of the growing tips can be taken in summer. You will need to keep the leaves moist, but the soil on the dry side. The cuttings develop best under a misting unit with a little bottom heat of 60°F.

MEDICINAL USES _____

There are few strong traditions of medicinal use for tarragon.
Because its name comes from the word "little dragon," it was
thought to have considerable power to heal bites and stings from
snakes, serpents, and other venomous creatures. It had the
reputation of being a friend to the head, lungs, heart and liver.
It was formerly used for toothache relief because it acts as an
anesthetic. Tarragon oil contains estragole, a volatile ether. A wad
of leaves would be heated gently with an iron and then cooled and
placed in the affected area of the mouth. Arab physicians gave
patients tarragon to chew on before giving them unpleasant-tasting
medicine. Egyptians used tarragon as a tasty medicinal herb.
Although not as powerful as fennel, it does relieve flatulence, colic,
and nausea. It has been used as a poultice for rheumatism and gout
with success. It has also shown to be useful as an anti-fungal
property.

A compound called rutin contained in tarragon is being studied as
a cancer preventative. Rutin can also help regulate blood pressure.
Cooking or boiling tarragon dissipates the potassium, so it's better
to eat tarragon raw if you are looking for help with high blood
pressure. Tea from the leaves is said to overcome insomnia. Its
chemical properties act as an astringent, and it has been said
tarragon prevents fatigue.

 OTHER USES _____

Chewing fresh tarragon leaves sweetens the breath and numbs the
tongue by giving off a camphor-anise taste. It also stimulates the
appetite. When planted among vegetables, tarragon will enhance
their growth. It can protect foodstuffs as an antioxidant. It's also a
good source of potassium, a mineral that helps prevent high blood
pressure and strokes. One tablespoon of dried tarragon contains
145 milligrams of potassium.

 CULINARY USES _____

The flavor of tarragon includes hints of anise, licorice, mint, hay, pine, pepper, and turpentine. Somehow, its taste is still harmonious. The green shoots are both warm and cool to the palette. Cooking brings out the warming quality while uncooked leaves are cooling, clean and refreshing. A somewhat mysterious property in the leaf can be noted by chewing on a fresh leaf. You may experience a numb feeling on your tongue. Although tarragon is popularly associated with vinegar and fish (especially lobster) because of its licorice character it is particularly suited to both. Tarragon deserves a wider role in the kitchen. Tarragon's exciting flavor is classic in sauce, from Bearnaîse, and Hollandaise to tartar. Tarragon can be dominating and overshadow or fight with other flavors. Tarragon actually tastes best on its own or with lemon or the classic fines herbes, parsley, chervil and chives. (See the Recipe Section for this combination.) The stronger herbs of rosemary, sage and thyme do not harmonize well with it. Since heat brings out its flavor, beware of using too much. Tarragon is the Mercedes of the culinary herb world. Cooks of all levels covet this most enticing and distinctive flavor. This kitchen legend is an appetite stimulant. Of course, just thinking about a dish prepared with tarragon makes me hungry!

Tarragon is excellent with eggs, souffle´s, cheeses and sauces of all kinds. I use it with cottage cheese, sour cream, yogurt and even tofu. My favorite uses are on poultry and in poultry stuffing. See the tarragon/chicken salad recipe in the Recipes Section for a wonderful example. A light sprinkling goes well with many simply prepared vegetables like peas, spinach, tomatoes, carrots and potatoes. It stars in fish and seafood dishes, especially with oily fish such as salmon and cod. In various salads, like rice, pasta, potato, green and coleslaw, it adds depth and new culinary taste. Many salad dressings, especially French dressings, are made with tarragon. In continental cookery the use of tarragon is advised to temper the coolness of other herbs like chervil, chives, parsley and lemon balm. Use this spicy herb in game, liver, kidneys, veal and rabbit. It, of course, gives a unique flavor to vinegar and mustards. For easy mustard, just add tarragon to Dijon. I make tarragon herb butter, mayonnaise and oil as well as vinegar and mustard.

Saute' mushrooms in butter and add chopped tarragon at the end of the cooking time. This is a great treat over steak or baked potatoes. Add tarragon to long-cooking soups and stews during the last fifteen minutes only. Saute' boneless chicken breasts with walnuts in peanut oil and toss in chives and tarragon about five minutes before the chicken is done. Before roasting a chicken, stuff tarragon and garlic slivers under the breast and leg skin. Create a fish salad by combining poached haddock, crumbled feta cheese, pitted green olives, and fresh tarragon. Dress with tarragon vinaigrette. Try tarragon in veal Marengo. I like tarragon in tomato soup and fish chowders but don't add this herb with a heavy hand. Avoid bringing out its bitter side by cooking it too long. I also like it in consomme' and in vegetable juice. Tarragon goes well with strong and pungent vegetables such as onions, leeks, cauliflower, cabbage, broccoli and brussel sprouts. Try it on artichokes, tomatoes, carrots, asparagus, mushrooms, and peas instead of basil or dill. Use one teaspoon of minced fresh tarragon per recipe for four. Add right before serving so it doesn't become bitter. Use a tablespoon of fresh tarragon in a green salad and dress with lemon juice and olive oil. Use tarragon vinaigrette (see recipes) on cooked beets. Tarragon seems to enliven everything edible in the kitchen other than desserts (with the exception of cheese desserts.)

 **RECIPES**

Tarragon Brew for Indigestion
1 oz. fresh tarragon leaves
1 stick vanilla
12 oz. sugar
½ pint of 40-50% alcohol (Vodka or Gin)

Mix and infuse this mixture for a month. Strain and drink after a heavy meal when indigestion occurs.

Tarragon -Lemon Vinegar

I generally do not choose distilled white vinegar for herbal or fruit vinegars because the flavor is too harsh and overcomes the gentle herb flavors. You may choose, however, white wine vinegar, apple cider vinegar, red wine vinegar, rice wine vinegar (the white, not red or black). Choose vinegar that you like even without the herbs. If it is unpleasant before herbs are added, it will still be unpleasant later. Buy vinegar by the gallon because it is so much cheaper. Four Monks™ is a good brand. The use of one cup of fresh herbs to two cups vinegar will give you strongly flavored vinegar. If using dried herbs (or flowers), use one-half cup dried to two cups vinegar. All flavorings need to be covered by the vinegar so they do not mold.

Pick leafy stalks of tarragon before the hot sun has drawn out the aromatic oils, and pack them in a clean, glass jar. Leaves may be removed from the stems if you wish, but this is an extra step that I don't feel is necessary. Place three to four strips of lemon zest (the colored portion of the rind only) in the jar. Fill the jar with white wine vinegar, which has been heated to just below a simmer, or about 180° F. Infuse the contents in a sunny location with a nonmetallic lid. After about four weeks, decant and strain the vinegar into a bottle and add a clean cork. The tarragon from the bottle can still be used for other recipes.

Tarragon Vinaigrette

2 Tbs. chopped fresh tarragon
1 Tbs. chopped chives with blossoms
3 Tbs. sherry vinegar
3 Tbs. rice wine vinegar
½ cup good quality olive oil
Salt and freshly ground pepper to taste

Place in a jar and shake vigorously. Store any excess in the refrigerator.

Tarragon Salad Dressing

¼ cup olive oil
3 Tbs. white-wine vinegar
1 Tbs. light mayonnaise
1 tsp. tarragon leaves, crushed
1 tsp. salt (optional)
¼ tsp. ground black pepper

In a small bowl, combine oil, vinegar, mayonnaise, tarragon, salt and pepper. Makes one-half cup.

Tarragon-Vanilla Salad Dressing

(Makes 2-½ cups)

This creamy, low-fat dressing lends itself to salad greens, cooked or raw vegetable combinations, pasta and grain salads, or as a dipping sauce for crudités or steamed artichoke leaves. It may be prepared with low-fat mayonnaise instead of yogurt for a richer flavor.

1 ½ tsp. garlic, crushed
1 tsp. Dijon mustard
1 Tbs. each chopped fresh tarragon, oregano, and basil
2 Tbs. chopped fresh parsley
1 ½ tsp. sugar
Few drops of vanilla extract
1 Tbs. fresh lemon juice
½ tsp. salt
Dash Tabasco
1 cup buttermilk
1 cup nonfat or low-fat plain yogurt

In a medium bowl, combine all the ingredients, whisking until smooth. Adjust and season with salt and pepper and/or lemon juice. Refrigerate until needed. The flavor improves upon standing and the dressing will keep for up to a week.

Tarragon Pesto
(Pesto means to pound)

½ cup coarsely chopped tarragon leaves
1 ¼ cup chopped fresh parsley (including stems)
1 clove garlic
¼ cup toasted almonds
½ cup fresh Parmesan cheese
½ cup olive oil to make a paste. (See directions for dill pesto.)

Creamy Tarragon Sauce
This recipe may be used as a salad dressing, on vegetables or as a sauce over cooked chicken, fish or eggs.

½ tsp. fresh tarragon
1 Tbs. Dijon mustard
1 Tbs. mayonnaise (low-fat or regular)
1 Tbs. olive oil
1 Tbs. white wine vinegar (or rice vinegar)
½ cup yogurt

Whisk together all the ingredients except the yogurt. After the mixture is well-blended, stir yogurt in carefully. Let mellow for an hour before serving.

Bearnáise Sauce
Makes 1 cup (use on roast beef, steaks, and hamburgers)

¼ cup tarragon vinegar
2 Tbs. minced shallots
2 Tbs. finely chopped tarragon
¼ tsp. white pepper
3 large egg yolks
1 cup melted butter

Mix vinegar, shallots, tarragon and pepper together in a small saucepan. Cook over high heat until mixture has reduced to one or two tablespoons. Transfer contents of saucepan to blender or food processor. Add egg yolks and process briefly. With machine running, slowly add cooled melted butter in a steady stream and blend until mixture thickens. Serve immediately.

Tarragon Aioli Sauce
(Makes 2 cups)

8-10 peeled garlic cloves
2 egg yolks at room temperature
Salt and white pepper to taste
Juice of 1 lemon
1 tsp. Dijon mustard
1 ½ cups oil, room temperature (half peanut, half-olive)
2 tsp. crushed tarragon

Crush garlic in blender or kitchen processor. Beat egg yolks in small bowl until frothy. Add salt and pepper, lemon juice and mustard to bowl then add to blender/processor. Slowly add the oil in a steady stream until sauce is shiny and holds its shape. Stir in the tarragon.

Tarragon Mustard Sauce
(Makes about 2 cups)

⅓ cup dry, white wine
1 shallot, sliced
A few peppercorns
¼ cup Dijon mustard
1 cup cream
2 Tbs. minced fresh tarragon

Place wine, shallot and peppercorns in saucepan. Reduce over low heat about five-to-ten minutes until only two tablespoons remain, and strain. Return the wine to the pan; discard shallot and peppercorns. In a small bowl, stir two tablespoons mustard into the cream; add the remaining mustard and stir into the reduced wine. Add the minced tarragon and cook at a light simmer for five minutes. over medium heat. Sauce will thicken slightly. Add salt and pepper to taste. Serve with pork loin, ham steak or poultry.

Tarragon Flavored Vodka
Two 4-inch sprigs of fresh tarragon
1 ½ cups of 80 proof vodka

Rinse and dry tarragon sprigs. Place in bottle of vodka, cover and allow the flavor to mellow at room temperature for 24 hours. Taste to see if it's strong enough; if not, steep for another 24 hours. Remove sprigs of tarragon and place vodka in freezer. It will become syrupy. Serve in one-ounce liqueur glasses with salmon, trout or other smoked fish.

Fines Herbés Mix
1 Tbs. chervil
1 Tbs. parsley
1 Tbs. chives
1 Tbs. tarragon

Use all fresh or all dried herbs in equal portions.
Add to egg or tuna salad sandwiches.

Crab Stuffed Avocados
(Serves 6 as an appetizer)

½ lb. crab meat (or imitation crab meat)
1 medium tomato, diced
1 stalk celery, diced
1 tsp. fresh tarragon, minced
⅓ cup mayonnaise, or tarragon aioli
3 avocados, halved, seeded and peeled

Combine crabmeat, tomato, celery, tarragon and mayonnaise. Blend together well and spoon into avocado halves.

Tarragon Deviled Eggs in Celery or Belgian Endive
(Serves 6 as an appetizer)

6 large eggs
¼ cup sour cream or yogurt
2 tsp. minced tarragon
2 tsp. Dijon-style mustard
1 tsp. tarragon vinegar
½ tsp. paprika
2 dashes of cayenne pepper
Salt
Capers
Celery stalks or Belgian endive leaves.

Hard-cook the eggs, peel, and cool them. Rub them through a medium sieve into a bowl. Add the sour cream, tarragon, mustard, vinegar, paprika, and cayenne pepper. Season with salt. Wash the celery stalks or Belgian endive leaves and dry well. Fill the vegetable pieces with the egg mixture using a pastry bag or a spoon. Garnish with capers and chill before serving.

Tarragon Pickles
(Makes 8 one-half pints)

2 ½ lb. scrubbed tiny pickling cucumbers
⅓ cup kosher salt
8 ½ cup cold water
2 ½ cup tarragon vinegar or tarragon lemon vinegar
1 Tbs. sugar
16 very small white pickling onions, peeled but with ends intact
16 tarragon sprigs, about two inches long
8 garlic cloves, peeled
8 small bay leaves
8 small dried hot red peppers
32 peppercorns

Trim off the stem ends of the cucumbers, rinse and drain. Place them in a large bowl with the salt and enough water to just cover, about 6 cups. Let them stand in a cool place for 6 hours or overnight. Drain the cucumbers well. Combine vinegar, 2 ½ cup water, and sugar in a non-corrosive saucepan and bring to a boil. Have ready eight sterilized, hot half-pint canning jars with lids. Fill the jars with drained cucumbers, layering the onions, herbs, and spices in between. Each jar should have two onions, two tarragon sprigs, one clove garlic, one bay leaf, one hot pepper and four peppercorns. Pour the boiling vinegar and water into each jar to one-quarter inch from the top. Wipe the rim of each jar and seal. Let the jars cool. Store any unsealed jars in the refrigerator and use within two weeks. Store sealed jars three to four weeks in a cool dark place before serving.

Chicken, Cashew and Tarragon Salad Sandwich
(Makes 4 sandwiches)

2 cups of roasted, de-boned chicken (breast and thigh meat chopped in one-half inch cubes
½ cup of chopped green onions, including some of the green tops
½ cup chopped celery, including some of the leaves
1 hard-boiled egg, chopped
1 Tbs. fresh tarragon chopped (or 1 tsp. dried)
Salt and pepper to taste
Enough mayonnaise to make a slightly moist stuffing

Combine all of the ingredients and stir lightly. Use on sandwiches with fresh lettuce leaves or sprouts, or stuff in hollowed-out tomatoes.

Shrimp and Corn Bisque with Tarragon
(Serves 6-8)
Crab, oysters, or scallops may be used instead of, or in addition to the shrimp in this soup.

4 Tbs. butter
1 cup thinly sliced celery
1 cup thinly sliced green onion
1 large clove garlic, minced
4 Tbs. flour
1 cup dry, white wine

4 cups defatted, chicken stock
Few drops of vanilla
1 ½ Tbs. chopped fresh tarragon
2 Tbs. chopped fresh sweet marjoram
3 large bay leaves
1 cup heavy cream
1 tsp. salt
⅛ tsp. ground white pepper
⅛ tsp. cayenne pepper
2 cups small corn kernels, fresh or frozen
1 ½ lb. peeled and deveined shrimp, cut in small pieces
⅝ to 1 cup sherry or vermouth
Chopped parsley or tarragon, for garnish

Melt the butter in a large heavy saucepan. Saute´the celery, green
onion, and garlic until soft but not brown. Sprinkle the flour over
the vegetables and stir to mix well. Add the wine and stock,
whisking to blend. Bring to a boil and add the vanilla, tarragon,
marjoram, and bay leaves. Reduce the heat and simmer 20-25 min,
or until the sharpness of the wine has disappeared and flavors have
mellowed. Add the cream and remaining ingredients. Raise the
heat to medium-high and cook three-to-five minutes until heated
through. Adjust the seasonings if necessary. Remove the bay leaves
before serving.

Mushroom-Tarragon Soup
(Makes 4 servings)

1 lb. mushrooms, rinsed and ends trimmed (any type or a
combination)
4 cups chicken stock
¼ cup lightly packed fresh tarragon leaves
¾ cup whipping cream

Set aside two mushrooms. In a blender or food processor, whirl
remaining mushrooms, broth and two tablespoons of the tarragon,
half at a time, until mushrooms are finely chopped. Pour into a
three-to-four quart pan. Bring to a boil over high heat, and then
simmer, covered, until flavors mellow, about ten minutes. Stir in

person when she's with people, a cat when she is with Ivan and Connie Chung, and a bird with her latest two friends. She has even tried to fly like them but, of course, always falls on her face. Tarragon really is my favorite herb and my favorite 'people puppy' as well.

NOTES

GLOSSARY OF TERMS _____

Aioli: A sauce similar to mayonnaise. See tarragon.

Annual: This type of plant completes its life cycle in one growing season; going from seed to flower and back to seed. An example is summer savory.

Antibacterial: This is a substance that is effective against bacteria.

Antibiotic: This is a substance produced by a microorganism that is capable of killing or inhibiting the growth of bacteria or other microorganisms.

Anticoagulant: This substance hinders blood clotting.

Anti-flatulent: This is a substance that rids the digestive tract of excessive gas.

Anti-fungal: This is a substance that clears the body of fungal irritations such as athlete's foot.

Anti-inflammatory: This substance treats conditions of localized heat, redness, swelling and pain, which is a result of irritation, injury or infections.

Antioxidant: This is a chemical compound or substance that inhibits oxidation and cell damage by free radicals.

Antiseptic: This is a substance that destroys bacteria; usually applied to the skin to prevent infection.

Antispasmodic: This is a medicine that relieves or prevents involuntary muscle spasms or cramps such as those occurring in epilepsy, painful menstruation, intestinal cramping, or 'charley horses.'

Aromatics: These are contained in plants, drugs, or medicines with a spicy scent and pungent taste. Among the aromatic plants are ginger, sweetflag, the mints, lavenders, household herbs such as peppers, cloves, nutmeg, etc. The essential oils in these plants, added to medicines, make them palatable.

Astringent: This is a substance that causes dehydration, tightening or shrinking of tissues and is used to stop bleeding, close skin pores and tighten muscles.

Axil: This is the angle of a plant between the upper surface of a leafstalk, flower stalk, branch or similar part and the stem or axis from which it arises.

Biennial: This type of plant completes its life cycle in two physiological growing seasons (usually 2 years); example is parsley. The seeds are produced on flower stalks in the second growing season.

Binomial Nomenclature: This is the botanical classification system that is the scientific way of naming plants using a two-name system; genus and species. The International Congress of Botanical Nomenclature controls plant names. The full botanical system includes units of Kingdom, Division, Sub-division, Class, Subclass, Order, Family, Genus, Species, Botanical Variety, and Cultivar. Every binomial has meaning and is significant. See also Genus and Species.

Bolt: Annual plants that grow quickly to flowering stage at the expense of good overall development sometimes bolt. This happens most often when plants are set out too late in the year or when unseasonably hot weather rushes the growth.

Botulism: This is an extremely dangerous food poisoning that can cause nerve damage and even death.

Bouquet Garni´: This is a collection of various herbs (usually thyme, bay and marjoram) tied up with string or in cheesecloth and used in cooking stews, poultry and fish dishes.

Bracts: This leaf-like plant part is located either below a flower or on the stalk of a flower cluster.

Bruising: This is a method of releasing the volatile oil within a seed, leaf or stem when using in culinary, medicinal or cosmetic form. This bruising can be done by slightly mashing the herb part in a mortar and pestle, or the leaves can be crushed gently in the hand.

B.t.: Bacillus thuringiensis is a bacterial insecticide that will work nicely if applied when caterpillars are young. B.t. is a stomach poison, not a contact poison.

Calyx: A part of the flower petal.

Carminative: This is a substance that checks the formation of gas and helps dispel whatever gas has already formed in the intestinal tract.

Cathartics: These are medicines, which relieve constipation. Laxatives stimulate and quicken peristaltic action, while cathartics stimulate the secretions of the intestines, often with strong physical manifestations.

Chiffonade: This is a way of cutting plant material that is faster and simpler than individual cuts. Fold several sorrel leaves together, roll them up and slice in small rings.

Chlorosis: This is a condition of yellowing of plant leaves that can be caused by insufficient iron or several other reasons.

Colic: This is spasmodic pain affecting smooth muscles, such as the intestines, gallbladder, or urinary tract.

Compress: To make a compress fold a cloth and moisten it with an herbal infusion, and then apply to the skin. It is often used to accelerate healing of wounds or muscle injuries. A cold compress is sometimes used for headaches. Infusions, decoctions and tinctures diluted with water can all be used for a compress and the pad can be soft cotton or linen, cotton ball, or surgical gauze.

Cotyledon: These are the first set of leaves that appear on a plant but are not the true leaves of the plant species.

Cough Syrup: See syrup, medicinal.

Crystallized flowers: This is a process of preserving flower petals by using an egg white and fine sugar wash mixture and then drying the petals thoroughly. See the borage chapter.

Cultivar, cv.: This is a short version of 'cultivated variety,' a botanical term used to explain a variation within a species, which is only maintained in cultivation. These cultivars are singled out because of their particular fragrance, color or form. Naming a variety of cultivar means adding a third or fourth word to the Latin genus and species: Salvia officinalis 'Aurea'.

Cuttings, Stem: These are portions of the stems, sometimes called "slips," that can be induced to form roots and develop into new plants, identical to the "mother" plant.

Damping Off: This soil-borne fungal disease attacks seedlings at the soil line and kills them. Use a sterile soilless medium to prevent this from occurring.

Decoction: This is a method of preparing a medicinal. It involves a more vigorous extraction of a plant's active ingredients than an infusion and is used for roots, barks, twigs, and some berries. Extracting an herbal essence by boiling roots, bark or other substances does this. Boil these parts for two to three minutes and simmer ten minutes. Decoctions may be applied externally or taken internally as a strong tea. As with infusions, the standard quantity should be made fresh each day and is enough for three doses.

Dehydration: This form of preserving herbs may be done by using the sun (solar), a commercial dehydrator, a conventional oven, microwave oven, or by hanging the herbs in bunches. (See: Living Foods Dehydrator)

Demulcents: These are medicines that are soothing to the intestinal tract, usually of an oily or mucilaginous nature. Glycerin and olive oil, are well-known examples.

Dermatitis: This is an inflammation of the skin.

Desiccant: This is a substance that has a high affinity for water and is used as a drying agent.

Diaphoretic: This is a medicine or agent that produces perspiration.

Diazanon: This is a commercial pesticide that is safe on plants.

Diuretics: These are medicines that tend to increase the secretion and discharge of urine.

Dyspepsia: This is a medical term for indigestion.

Emetics: These are agents that cause vomiting.

Emollients: These are similar to demulcents, but emollients are materials that soothe the skin rather than the internal membranes.

Espalier: This is the art of growing a plant in one plane, against a wall, trellis, or other flat support. These plants can also be trained against a balcony, fence, and screen on a terrace or in a freestanding container.

Essential Oils: These are the concentrated vital essences of aromatic plants. They are a great boon to present-day potpourri blends for adding intensity and depth to a fragrant mixture, or in perfumery and aromatherapy. This volatile material derived from a plant usually bears the aroma or flavor of that plant. These oils must be used with discretion to avoid dominating subtler scents. Oils won't mix with water but they are soluble in many organic solvents. Being volatile, they evaporate rapidly at room temperature.

Essiac: This is a tea that has been used in Canada for over sixty years to treat cancer made from burdock root, sheep sorrel, Turkish rhubarb, and slippery elm bark. Rene Caisse (Essiac spelled backwards) learned of the recipe from a woman who used it to cure her cancer. An Ojibway herbalist was the source of her information.

Expectorant: This is a substance that, taken internally, helps the body expel phlegm through coughing, sneezing, or spitting and enables a patient to bring up and spit out excessive secretions which accumulate in lungs and windpipe.

Facial Steam: This is a method for deep cleansing of the face. Bruised herbs are brought to a boil in water and the face, under a towel, is placed near the steam when it is cool enough to tolerate.

Fish Emulsion: A liquid fertilizer, such as Alaska Fish Fertilizer™, is an organic method of fertilization.

Flatulence: This is a gas in the stomach or bowels. Fennel, dill and sage are helpful remedies. See also carminative.

Genus: This category in binomial nomenclature ranks below Family and above Species. It is used to describe a similar group of plants. Each genus in the plant kingdom has a unique name. It is common practice to talk about plants by their genus, or generic name; i.e. Salvia officinalis 'Aurea.' Salvia is the genus.

Gingivitis: This is an inflammation of the gums.

Heeling Plants: This term refers to a means of preventing roots of bare-rooted plants from drying out before you can set them out in the garden. Dig a trench and lay the plant on its side so that roots are in the trench, then cover roots with soil, sawdust, or other material, moistened to keep roots damp.

Herbaceous: This term describes a plant with a non-woody top. Green and leaf-like in appearance and texture, these plants will die down to ground level during the cold dormant season.

Hybrid: This is a plant that is a cross between two species; usually forced and has mixed origin or composition.

Infusion: This product is made in much the same way as tea and used in a medicinal way. The water should be just off the boil since vigorously boiling water disperses valuable volatile oils in the steam. Use this method for flowers and the leafy parts of plants. The standard quantity should be made fresh each day and is sufficient for three doses. Drink the tea hot or cold after infusing for ten minutes.

Insecticidal Soap: A product used as an insecticide that is organic such as, Safer™.

IPM: Integrated Pest Management: Integrated pest management is a technique of pest and disease control that works by establishing tolerable levels of crop damage from a particular pest or disease. Once the goal is set for the size of the crop, cultural, physical, biological, and in limited amounts, chemical controls are integrated to manage pests at a tolerable level. Herbs help maintain a population of beneficial insects that attack or parasitize aphids, caterpillars and a host of other pests. Tiny helpful wasps and hover flies especially love the dill and fennel plants. Bt. (bacillus thuringiensis) is a bacterium that kills larvae and caterpillars from budworms to cabbage loppers and an effective insecticidal soap for aphids.

Knot Garden: This is a design made with low compact herbs, such as sage, in an over-and-under lapping pattern within a defined space to create a symmetrical pattern.

Living Foods Dehydrator: This company makes the wooden dehydrator that I have used for 25 years. I recommend it to all my students in food preservation and herb drying classes. Address: PO Box 546, Fall City, Washington 98024.

Lotion: This is a water-based mixture that is applied to the skin as a cooling or soothing remedy to relieve irritation or inflammation. Alcohol-based mixtures such as tinctures can be added to lotions to increase the cooling effect.

Mulch: Mulch can assist with weed control, conserve moisture, improve the soil, provide a path and unify and improve a garden. These might include, black plastic for weed control, straw (with no herbicides or pesticides), peat to improve soil, bark retains moisture and suppressed weeds, large leaves of Angelica and Comfrey, will gradually break down and improve soil texture if cast down between plants. Worms love it.

Narcotic: This is a substance that causes stupor and numbness.

Nematodes: A worm of the division, Nematoda, has an unsegmented, threadlike body. Many of these are parasitic. Nematodes may be a pest or used as a preventive.

Nervines: These are tonics for the nerves and may be stimulating, sedating, or relaxing.

Neuralgia: This pain occurs along a nerve.

Pearls: Slugs (snails) lay tiny eggs in masses that look like pearls. Seek and destroy.

Perennial: These plants grow three or more seasons in their appropriate climates. Sage is an example of a perennial herb.

Petiole: The stalk by which a leaf is attached to the stem; a leafstalk.

pH: Potential for hydrogen: pH (pronounced pee-aach) is a noun in chemistry that measures the acidity or alkalinity of a solution (soil). Measurements are from 1 to 14; 7 is neutral: the higher alkaline the higher the number 7.5, 8.0 etc.; the lower the number the more acidity 6.8, 5.7, 4.5 etc.

Phlegm: This is a stringy, thick mucus secreted by the respiratory system.

Pot Herb: Pot herbs are so called because the leaves, and sometimes the rootstock of certain plants, were used in nourishing broth and also as vegetables, as well as having their place, raw, in salads. These pot herbs were gathered growing wild along hedgerows, in fields and in woods, and were also cultivated in early gardens, especially in monastery gardens, which are said to be the forerunners of today's kitchen gardens. Besides providing something to eat, it was considered necessary to cleanse the blood after a winter diet of the warming, heavy food needed for cold weather.

Potpourri: This French word means a blend of spicy flowers or a medley. The French word for pot, and 'pourrir' means to rot. A mixture of sweet-scented herbs - lemon verbena, anise hyssop, bay - can be used to make potpourri. Ingredients, including spices, are usually kept in a whole or semi-whole state. Essential fragrant oils capture the fragrant oils of flowers and herbs. Fixative absorbs the oil's essence and preserves its aroma for many months or years. Orrisroot, which comes from the Florentine Iris, is the most common fixative.

Poultice: This has a similar action as a compress, but the whole herb rather than a liquid extract is applied. Poultices are generally applied hot but cold fresh leaves can be just as suitable. Chop fresh herbs in a food processor for a few seconds and boil in a little water for two to five minutes. Boil the fresh herb, squeeze out any surplus liquid and spread it on the affected area. Smooth a little oil on the skin first, to prevent the herb from sticking. Apply gauze or cotton strips to hold the poultice carefully in place.

Psoriasis: This is a skin disorder of unknown cause and is more annoying than dangerous.

Purgatives: This term is generally synonymous with cathartics.

Roux: This is a French word for mixing together flour and fat, cooked and used as a thickening.

Rugose: This is a term for a leaf covered with wrinkles or corrugated. These plants have a rough surface with strongly veined leaves.

Sachet: This can be made for the bath by tying handfuls of dried leaves or petals in squares of cheesecloth; lovage is excellent. Sachet ingredients are generally crumbled or ground as opposed to potpourri which is left in a whole state.

Sedatives: These are drugs, which tend to calm or tranquilize the nervous system.

Seed Savings: Abundant Life Seeds, PO Box 772, 1029 Lawrence St., Port Townsend, WA 98368 or United Plant Savers, PO Box 420, East Barre, VT 05649

Species: This is a plant comprising all the individuals that share common attributes and are capable of inter-breeding freely with one another but not with a member of another species. Any number from one to hundreds of species that are similar in meaningful way can be combined into a genus.

Sterile Soil: This is a mixture that contains little or no nutrients, minerals, phosphorous, nitrogen, etc., and is usually used to establish cuttings.

Stimulants: These are substances that temporarily increase mental or physical activity. They are a tonic rather than a narcotic. They increase or quicken the various functional actions of the body such as hastening digestion, raising body temperature or heart rate. The substance does this quickly, unlike a tonic, which stimulates general health over a period of time.

Stolon: This is a stem that creeps along the surface of the ground, taking root at intervals and forming new plants where it roots.

Stomachic: This is a substance that is beneficial or stimulating to the digestive system.

Syrup, Medicinal: Honey or unrefined sugar can be used to preserve infusions and decoctions, and syrup makes an ideal cough remedy; honey is particularly soothing. The added sweetness also disguises the flavor or more unpleasant-tasting herbs, such as motherwort. Syrups can also be used to flavor medicines for children.

Tender Perennial: This is the opposite of a hardy perennial and denotes low tolerance to freezing temperatures.

Tisane: This is an old-fashioned name for tea that is made from an infusion and generally drunk for medicinal purposes.

Tonics or Tonic Herbs: These are often referred to as 'bitters' in old books and frequently act as stimulants. They give tone and vigor to the body's systems, providing a general feeling of well being. These substances invigorate or strengthen the system.

Topical: This is the local administration of an herbal remedy, e.g. to the skin or eye.

Transpiration: This is the act of transpiring vapor containing waste products through the stomata of plant tissue.

Umbel: This is a flat-top or rounded flower cluster in which the individual flower stalks arise from about the same point as in the carrot, dill or fennel.

Variety, var.: This is a fairly consistent, naturally occurring variation within a species of plants.

Volatile Oil: See Essential Oil.

Whorls: These are floral clusters in which each individual flower is attached by its own stem to a common point at the top of the stalk.

Zest: This is the colored portion of the skin of a citrus fruit; i.e. lemon, orange, lime. This does not include the pith, or white portion under the zest. The pith is very bitter and should not be used. To obtain only the zest of a fruit, use a potato peeler.

Index

ABOUT THE AUTHOR

Carol R. Peterson has been studying and using herbs for almost thirty years - long before it was popular. Not until the 1990's have others now understood the importance of these wonderful plants for their lives.

She is a teacher at several colleges and hospitals and lectures throughout the Pacific Northwest. With the release of her first book, **Herbs You Can Master: A Primer for Herbal Enthusiasts**, she was featured on several television shows and many, many radio programs throughout the United States and Canada. She has written numerous articles for newsletters, magazines and newspapers and has been featured in many newspapers around the country.

Carol is a Master Gardner and Food Advisor in King County, Washington. She is a member of the Herb Society of America, The International Herb Association and Book Publishers Northwest.

Carol and her husband Charles have two grown children and a small puppy, Miss Tarragon Peterson, who is Carol's only grandchild. They reside in Snoqualmie, Washington and have a greenhouse and one third of an acre for growing herbs the year around. Summers you will find Carol with guests and clients on a garden tour and serving a delightful and delicious herbal luncheon at the Peterson home. She also maintains a small herbal product line, consults with clients and students on herbal "cures" and plans herbal gardens for others.

Catch the new website at: **www.moreherbs.com.**

ORDER FORM

Postal Orders:

Mountain Garden Publishing, Inc.
PO Box 98
Snoqualmie, WA 98065

Telephone Orders: 425-888-0773

Please have your VISA or MasterCard Ready.

☐ **Herbs You Can Master**
Number of copies @ $13.95ea : _____

☐ **More Herbs You Can Master**
Number of copies @ $17.95ea : _____

Sales Tax: Washington Residents: Sales Tax: 8.2%

Shipping and Handling:

Book Rate: $2.50 for the 1st book,
$1.00 for each additional book.
Air Mail: $3.50 per book.

Shipping Total $: _____

Total $: _____

Autograph To? _____
Payment Type: _____

☐ Check Enclosed
☐ Credit Card ☐ **VISA** ☐ **MasterCard**

Card Number: _____
Name on Card: _____
Expiration Date: _____
Signature: _____